All God's People Are Ministers

All God's People Are Ministers

EQUIPPING CHURCH MEMBERS FOR MINISTRY

PATRICIA N. PAGE

Augsburg
MINNEAPOLIS

ALL GOD'S PEOPLE ARE MINISTERS
Equipping Church Members for Ministry

Scripture quotations are from the New Revised Standard Version Bible, copyright © 1989 by the Division of Christian Education of the National Council of the Churches of Christ in the United States of America. Used with permission.

Excerpts from "Sleep" are from *God Speaks* by Charles Peguy, copyright © 1943 Pantheon Books, Inc., and are reprinted by permission of Pantheon Books, a division of Random House, Inc.

"Washing the Dishes" is from *The Miracle of Mindfulness* by Thich Nhat Hanh, copyright © 1975, 1976 Thich Nhat Hanh, and is reprinted by permission of Beacon Press.

The diagram on page 83 is from *Charismata* by John Koenig, copyright © 1990 John Koenig, and is used by permission.

Cover design: Pollock Design Group

Library of Congress Cataloging-in-Publication Data

Page, Patricia N.
　　All God's people are ministers : equipping church members for
ministry / Patricia N. Page.
　　　　p.　　cm.
　　Includes bibliographical references.
　　ISBN 0-8066-2643-7 (alk. paper)
　　1. Lay ministry.　　I. Title.
BV677.P34　　　1993
253—dc20　　　　　　　　　　　　　　　　　　　　　93-19835
　　　　　　　　　　　　　　　　　　　　　　　　　　　　CIP

The paper used in this publication meets the minimum requirements of American National Standard for Information Sciences—Permanence of Paper for Printed Library Materials, ANSI Z329.48-1984. ∞™

Manufactured in the U.S.A.　　　　　　　　　　　　　　　　AF 9-2643

97　96　95　94　93　1　2　3　4　5　6　7　8　9　10

Contents

Introduction

Ministry has been a major concern of Christian churches throughout the world during the past forty years, and it continues to be a concern. Christians talk a lot about "What is ministry? Who does it? Where is it done?" An exciting and energizing part of this concern has been the discovery of the church's historic recognition of the "people of God," the *laos* (Gk., "people").

Yves Congar, a French Dominican theologian, produced a massive study of the theology of the laity in 1953; and Hendrik Kraemer, a Dutch Protestant theologian, wrote *The Theology of the Laity* in 1958.[1] Lay centers were established in Germany and Switzerland, and laity in Germany began the Kirchentag, a biannual week-long celebration of the ministry of God's people.

Vatican Council II (1962-65) has been very influential in the life of the whole Christian church in this century. The move from hierarchical to conciliar structures, the provision for the liturgy in vernacular languages, the encouragement of Bible reading and Bible study, the openness to other Christian bodies and other religions—all are still working themselves out in both hopeful and painful ways. The emphasis in this Council on the biblical model of the church as the whole people of God has made this model a most effective symbol for all Christian bodies.

Now "lay ministry" is recognized as important to all Christians. Pope John Paul II, in October 1987, led a World Synod of Roman Catholic bishops in conferring about the ministry of the laity. Churches such as the United Methodist Church, in its 1988 Book of Discipline, and the Episcopal Church, in its 1976 Prayer Book Catechism, have reworked statements of their beliefs to reflect the primacy of the general ministry of all Christians. The recently merged Evangelical Lutheran Church in America has a Department on Ministry in Daily Life in its Division for Ministry. Seminaries and theological colleges provide courses specifically prepared for laity.

The marked increase in renewal movements, many of which have been lay led and some very anticlerical, is seen throughout the church. The charismatic movement that has spread throughout the Christian church around the world in the twentieth century has been, in part, a reaction to the more formal organization of church life and practice and has released many laypersons for ministry.

Everywhere, it seems—in Chicago, Australia, Shanghai, and Zambia—lay people are doing ministry in worship, in teaching, in caring, and in service. In some instances laypersons are taking on many of the administrative and professional pastoral roles in the church because of the lack of persons in ordained leadership. Phrases such as "mutual," "total," or "shared" ministry suggest how clergy are allowing laity to share in their traditional ministry. Some church bodies are rewriting their practices to authorize or "ordain" laypersons for a variety of functions within the church. As this view of laity in ministry has changed, so there has come a new emphasis for the ordained ministry on its role as "enabler of lay ministry."

With this tremendous increase of emphasis on "lay ministry" in the church everywhere, the question remains "What is the ministry of the people of God in this century and the next?"

People are struggling with this question. In one congregation, a visiting preacher talked about the ministry of laypersons in all the different places they find themselves, hour by hour and day by day. The congregation nodded in agreement, for this was a church with a great deal of lay involvement in all parts of its life—liturgy, education, pastoral care, and outreach. The pastor encouraged all of this lay ministry and appreciated it, because he was working hard in the community and studying for a graduate degree. Almost the last person to greet the preacher was a tired-looking, middle-aged woman. She said:

> I did like your sermon about lay ministry. How much I wish I could do what you talked about! But right now my father is dying and I have to

take care of him. He needs all my time and my energy. After he dies, then I will be able to do lay ministry.

In another situation one person had this to say:

> I am an accountant. As an accountant I live for and with figures. They talk to me, and I am expected to make them talk to others; to translate deeds, situations, products, yes—and people, into statistics, figures, charts.
>
> I am also a manager responsible for a very wide area of activity. In small companies this is especially true. I cover Company Secretary, Safety, Health, Personnel, Insurance, Training, Administration, Service as well as Accounts.
>
> My last three jobs have all been for organizations losing more than £100,000 per year—one was losing £600,000. Therefore I am expected to change more, save more, analyze more.
>
> The key question is, does my job and particularly perhaps the bleakness of the profitability cause a conflict and dilemma with my Christian outlook?
>
> So far I have largely worked out my Christianity at work unaided. There are no obvious forums for discussion, or at least when they exist they rarely touch the workplace. Why should they? Our workplaces, status, responsibilities are diverse. Not everyone likes groups anyway.
>
> But work takes up 20–30 percent of our existence for almost fifty years of our life. Working out our discipleship in that arena is important.[2]

From the other side of the lay-clergy relationship, some persons who were applying for ordained ministry as a second career reflected on their experiences. One woman commented:

> I did lots of volunteer work in the church, but I became exhausted from all that, and no one recognized what I was doing was ministry. I want to be ordained so I can have a real ministry.

A man in the group said:

> I was a lawyer—and a good one. But I wanted to help people, and I found I could not do this in the practice of law. I want to be ordained so I can respond fully to God's call to me.

These comments suggest there is a chasm between the church's present affirmation of lay ministry and the struggle and frustration of Christian laypersons who are trying to be faithful followers of Jesus Christ in all areas of their lives.

Some years ago J. B. Phillips wrote a book entitled *Your God Is Too Small*. We need to say the same about much of the church's understanding of ministry today—"Your ministry is too small." Our limited understandings doom us to limiting greatly the church's mission in the world by wearing out the gifts and energies of a few people and by ignoring and even belittling the many ministries Christian people are already doing but do not connect with their Christian commitment.

Much of the work for the breakthrough to new understandings and practice of the ministry of God's people can and should take place in each local congregation of Christians, in the environments in which Christians worship, learn, converse, and plan their ministry. These environments need to be created and sustained in such a way that they kindle new vision in ministry and uphold the people as they journey.

Ordained and professional laypersons have a very great part to play in this breakthrough. The Epistle to the Ephesians identifies the reason for their ministry: God has given the gifts of apostle, prophet, evangelist, pastor, and teacher in the church precisely to "equip the saints for the work of ministry" (4:11-12).

However, often those to whom God has given these gifts do not know how to do "equipping." As the Right Reverend Oliver B. Garver (formerly suffragan bishop of Los Angeles, now retired) once said, "I don't think that most clergy in any culture know what to do with a committed layperson. . . . It is a little frightening to raise up a cadre of committed lay people, especially those caught on fire or alive outside the comfort of tradition and order."

This book is written to suggest some of the methods and resources that are available for those who have the responsibility and commitment to engage in strengthening the laity in ministry. For eight years Otto Bremer and I taught such a course in the Graduate School of Theology in Berkeley, California. The students were those intending both ordained and lay vocations in the church; some were already ordained or, as laity, carried pastoral responsibilities. They were Baptist, Roman Catholic, Presbyterian, Methodist, Lutheran, Alliance, United Church, Episcopalian, and Disciples of Christ. They came from all parts of the United States and from New Zealand, Switzerland, Liberia, Zimbabwe, Japan, and the Philippines.

These students found that this course helped them to:
- find some specific suggestions of ways to equip God's people for the work of ministry;
- begin to explore other ways of being "equippers" that were rooted in their own traditions and that used their own unique gifts;
- accept that their ministry of "equipping" is their primary vocation, that it is an ongoing, day-in-and-day-out ministry, requiring patience,

imagination, and the willingness to risk everything for the sake of God's kingdom.

My hope is that through this book many other leaders in the church may be helped in their own ministry. Keep these questions in mind as you read the book:

- What is my own theology of the ministry of the laity?
- How do I see myself using my unique gifts to fulfill the vocation of strengthening laity in ministry?

The breakthrough into new understandings and practice of ministry of all God's people can come only as we get a fresh vision and are renewed in our response to God's call to us.

The Exercises and Practical Helps at the back of the book may be used to enhance individual or group study. Each exercise is keyed to the portion of the book with which it may be used.

This book has grown out of the work of three persons. I carried the primary responsibility for directing the project and the writing. A lay professional in the Episcopal Church for many years, I served as religious educator in parishes and dioceses in North Carolina and Maine and as Episcopal chaplain at Smith College. From 1963 to 1973 I was the advisor in Christian Education in the Anglican Church in Zambia. I was the director of the National Institute of Lay Training for five years before going to Berkeley, California, to be professor of Education and director of Continuing Education in the Church Divinity School of the Pacific. I retired in 1989.

Gail Jones spent many hours with me planning the book. She did some of the writing in chapter 1 on baptism and in chapter 7 on the formation of the congregation for ministry. Gail is now director of Education and Training for the Education for Ministry Program of the University of the South, Sewanee, Tennessee. As a lay professional religious educator she has worked in community development projects and has been consultant on Ministry Development in the diocese of Olympia.

Beginning in 1982 Otto Bremer and I taught Strengthening Laity in Ministry, a course in the Graduate Theological Union of Berkeley, California. Bremer is a Lutheran clergyman with education in the field of ethics and values in business management. He has been a parish pastor. Now he lectures in ethics, economics, and management in colleges and universities and is active in the programs of the Graduate Theological Union Center for Ethics and Social Policy. Many of the ideas in this book have come from the work that Bremer and I did together, and he wrote portions on the strengthening of the ministry of persons in business.

1

God's Call to Ministry

Where can we begin to make the breakthrough into new understandings and practice of the ministry of all God's people? Better religious education, more workshops on gift identification, and better sermons encouraging laity to carry out their ministry in daily life are all needed. This book is concerned with all these areas. However, what is absolutely central and necessary for this breakthrough is a much more radical reformation of the understanding and perception of ministry than that now guiding the Christian community.

The Christian Testament tells us that this ministry is grounded fundamentally in the whole company of those who have committed themselves to follow God's call in Jesus Christ. It is a continuing process into which we are brought and through which we offer our own lives over and over again. Ministry is both corporate and personal. Ministry is not the things we do or the titles we hold; rather it is a bond between us and God and between us and the rest of God's people.

THE CALL OF THE COVENANT COMMUNITY

Each congregation of Christians is the local gathering that provides the framework for ministry. It is where persons are incorporated into the community of God's holy people, the community of the new covenant called church, and where they join in the ongoing Christian pilgrimage.

The Christian concept of being a community of faith grew out of Israel's experience of being a community in covenant with God. At Mount Sinai, God said, "If you obey my voice and keep my covenant, you shall be my treasured possession out of all the peoples. Indeed, the whole earth is mine, but you shall be for me a priestly kingdom and a holy nation" (Ex. 19:5-6). God engaged the people in a covenant for God's own purposes. God said this people was chosen "so that you may know and believe me and understand that I am he" (Isa. 43:10). The people of Israel knew they could trust this God who was making the covenant because they had "seen" what God "did to the Egyptians" and had experienced being borne "on eagles' wings" and being carried to God (Ex. 19:4). The history of the community of Israel[1] is a continuous story of God calling this people, their rebellion and failure to obey, their repentance, and God's persistent re-calling. Always there were some men and women, in many different walks of life, who in their own ministry tried to hold the community faithful to the covenant. God's covenant with the Israelites continued: "I have called you by name, you are mine" (Isa. 43:1).

Circumcision became the outward sign of the covenant relationship. Although this physical sign was administered only to males, through the enactment of this sign every Israelite was incorporated into God's holy people.

The Christian Scriptures tell us of God's people brought into the gathered community of Jesus Christ. The writer of 1 Peter, in what may have been a sermon at an early second-century baptism, told them: ". . . you are a chosen race, a royal priesthood, a holy nation, God's own people, in order that you may proclaim the mighty acts of him who called you out of darkness into his marvelous light" (1 Peter 2:9). Baptism was the outward sign and seal of this covenant to be God's people.

The universal priesthood of all believers is grounded in baptism. Every person is born again to be a witness (Acts 1:8) and a priest (1 Peter 2:9). R. H. Faulkner, in the *National Baptist Churchman's Handbook*, says, "All believers are not prophets and preachers, but all are priests unto God and witnesses unto Christ."[2] Faulkner goes on to describe the priest as the person in the middle, representing God to humanity and humanity to God. Therefore, the ministry of reconciliation, of persons to each other, to creation, and to God becomes the highest calling of the royal priesthood.

Baptism is always a sign of hope. This covenant community, the chosen race (*genos*), the royal priesthood, the holy nation (*ethnos*), God's own people (*laos*), is created for God's purposes. When ministry is perceived in the context of God's "plan for the fullness of time, to gather all things in him, things in heaven and things on earth" (Eph. 1:10), it rises above trivia and fad or frustration and burnout. Cyprian, writing to his friend Donatus from Carthage in A.D. 246 recalled his baptism: "I was born a new man . . . freedom and spiritual power given us . . . and given authority over the whole force of the enemy who attacks us!"[3]

Jesus' own baptism by John in the Jordan River was a beginning of this new covenant between God and humankind. It was the beginning of Jesus' own ministry, which continues through the covenant community. When Christians accept baptism, they become part of this ministry of Jesus. The apostle Paul told the Christians in Corinth, "Now you are the body of Christ and individually members of it" (1 Cor. 12:27).

The church in its universal and local life is the incorporating body for Christians. It is not easy for persons who are shaped by the individualism of Western culture to grasp the significance of this incorporation nor for the church to be empowered by the understanding of itself as a baptizing community. We need to recover and create ceremonies and practices that break open the significance of this act for the mission and ministry of community and persons.

The story of the early Christian church in Acts tells us that in the beginning about three thousand persons were baptized and others were continually being added to this number. They met together to hear "the apostles' teaching" and for "fellowship . . . the breaking of bread and the prayers" (Acts 2:41-42). As the body of Christ, they engaged in God's mission in the world; "they would sell their possessions and goods and distribute the proceeds to all, as any had need." And they "were praising God and having the goodwill of all the people" (vv. 45-46).

As the church grew beyond Jerusalem and incorporated more and more members, the practices for baptizing persons into the covenant community also were enriched. The people who were being instructed and formed to be Christians were called catechumens (*catechumen* comes from the Greek word meaning "to be instructed by mouth"). They were required to undergo a period of preparation, as long as three years, with continued instruction in the biblical writings and the creed of the community. The catechumens fasted before entering into their initiation rites late on the evening before Easter. Solemn promises and sensory and dramatic acts were all part of the rites.

Roman Catholic theologian Aidan Kavanagh describes the way in which a fourth-century boy, Euphemius, was received into the household of God.[4] The baptism began when the bishop entered the vestibule of the baptistry and said to the catechumens: "Take off your clothes." Baptism had a "gruff robustness." This passage in Christ from death to life was marked by "the language of the bathhouse and the tomb—not that of the forum and the drawing room." After the boy was rubbed all over with oil and led into the baptismal pool, the bishop said to him, "Euphemius: do you believe in God the Father, who created all of heaven and earth?" When Euphemius said, "I do," the deacon lifted him backwards into the rushing water and forced him under the surface. This immersion was repeated as he affirmed his belief in each phrase of the Apostles' Creed. As Euphemius and the other catechumens came up out of the water, expensive perfumed oil was poured over their heads, running down their bodies, a sign of the Holy Spirit, designating them as members of the royal priesthood. By this time the first rays of the sun had appeared and the whole community joined in the celebration of the Eucharist, the joyful thanksgiving of Christ's resurrection. Such a corporate public act gave power for ministry not only to those being initiated but also to the whole community.

Today the rites of initiation need to be done in comparable ways that can enlarge the image of the covenant community and give it direction for its service in God's mission. Practical decisions need to be made. A time and place for this rite should be chosen which make possible the participation of the community, for it is the whole community who does the baptizing; those who are ordained simply perform the actions and say the words of the rite on behalf of all God's people. In the Service of Baptism in the *Book of Common Prayer*, the people are expected to pray for each candidate, and when all have been baptized, the whole congregation says, "We receive you into the household of God. Confess the faith of Christ crucified, proclaim his resurrection, and share with us in his eternal priesthood."[5] From the beginning the Christian community has held that the use of water and of the name of the Trinity were the only two essential parts of the rite of initiation. Over the centuries these essentials have been rendered in different places and different ways. Each church, universally and locally, must explore and develop those ways that give meaning to this corporate act of initiation in its time and place and culture.

Each time this rite of initiation is practiced, the church is reinstituted and the community renews its covenant to participate in God's mission for the world. The responsibility for being that community lies with all its members, not just the ordained or appointed lay leaders. Baptism is an event to be celebrated greatly. Too often the Christian community goes all out to celebrate when one of its members is ordained, set apart for a particular ministry within the body, or when that person celebrates the anniversary of that setting apart. However, the community forgets or makes little of the rites and anniversaries of baptism. Yet the baptism of each Christian is the foundation for the ministry of the whole church!

The recovenanting that takes place in each rite of initiation gives clarity of purpose and therefore power to the Christian community. The metaphors of "chosen race, a royal priesthood, a holy nation, God's own people" suggest many routes in the journey of proclaiming "the mighty acts of him who called you out of darkness into his marvelous light" (1 Peter 2:9).

METAPHORS OF MINISTRY

God is continually calling this community to reach out beyond their present understandings of the covenant to recognize more profound perspectives. Just so did Jesus tell his frustrated fishermen-disciples to go out again into the deep waters if they would fill their nets with fish.

One way in which we can expand our understanding of the covenant community is through metaphors. The Bible is full of metaphors, powerful figures of speech in which we speak about one thing in terms that suggest another. By using metaphors in our liturgies and educational events, we discern new meanings for the things of which we speak. Through metaphors we discover unexpected understanding and responses to God's call to us.

The New Testament often uses the metaphor of *the kingdom of God* as the ultimate goal of God's mission. When Jesus was asked to read in the synagogue in Nazareth, he chose Isaiah 61:1-2, which describes the good news of deliverance for the poor, the captives, the blind, and the oppressed (see Luke 4:18-19). This is a description of the kingdom of God, the rule of God, which gives freedom and wholeness to all. Jesus told the people, "The time is fulfilled, and the kingdom of God has come near" (Mark 1:15). So the church, the body of Christ, takes on the mission and ministry of Jesus Christ to bring about the fullness of God's rule. We need to study Jesus' teaching and ways of bringing the kingdom so that we may understand this mission and ministry better. There is great potential for the community's mission in understanding itself as a preview of the kingdom of God. This mission can only be done by the ministry of each person in the locale where he or she lives.

Another way the New Testament describes the kingdom of God is Jesus' promise of *new life*, or *abundant life* (John 10:10; in the Gospel of John "kingdom of God" is used only twice, both times in stories of Jesus' meeting with government officials). Jesus came to bring abundant life. Sharing this life is the mission of the community that exists to carry on Jesus' ministry. We do not know entirely what this abundant life might be, but we do know that his ministry is not bound by the limits of what seems possible here and now. William Carey, one early missionary, caught the spirit of this ministry when he said, "Expect great things from God; attempt great things for God."[6] Who would have believed that the resolution of people in one city to walk rather than ride segregated buses would set in motion a movement that would change the whole pattern of American society? Or who would believe that candelit processions would lead to the collapse of the Iron Curtain, as they did in East Germany? The Christian community is challenged to envision what the abundant life might look like in the locale where it is planted and to support its members in ministry that can bring new life to all there.

A different metaphor is *citizens with the saints and also members of the household of God, built upon the foundation of the apostles and prophets* (Eph. 2:19-20). Through this metaphor we can explore what it means to be part of the great company of believers of every age and place. The material in chapters 2 and 3 in this book can be especially helpful to this exploration. We begin to see that as a part of the church we are part of something that has much broader dimensions than the group of people meeting in the stone building at the corner of Main and Broad Streets. Our ministry is a part of the ongoing life of this great fellowship, and it will be measured by the ultimate results, not just what may happen tomorrow or the next day. Each phrase given in this metaphor—citizens, saints, members of the household of God, foundation, apostles, prophets—can provoke in us new understandings of who we are and what we are supposed to be about.

The phrase *the gifted community* is both a metaphor of the church and a description of the reality of this community. God gives gifts to every person—talents, abilities, personality traits, special strengths and limitations, and circumstances. The Holy Spirit opens our eyes to discern our own gifts and those of others. The Holy Spirit leads us to recognize that these are gifts from God and are to be used for God's purposes. In chapter 7 we will suggest ways in which we can help each other in this discernment of gifts and in opening up the many possibilities for using these gifts in God's mission.

God has given and continues to give gifts to each person, and God does not want those gifts wasted. God's bounteous gifts stretch the community to find ways to use the gifts of each member in its mission. Paul was clear that the gifts were not given for individual use or glory. Rather, "to each is given the manifestation of the Spirit for the common good" (1 Cor. 12:7). The shape and the mission of each Christian communion, in its local and wider gatherings, becomes reformed as each person with his or her unique gifts is incorporated into the body. The metaphor, *the gifted community*, also challenges us to delve deeper into the implications of being a community created by God for God's purposes, as a gift to the world (see Eph. 1:3-14).

All members of the church are *God's beloved, called to be saints*. Very often we have thought of saints as special people who have achieved some great feat or demonstrated unusual gifts in ministry. However, when Paul wrote to the various churches, he addressed all the people as saints, for example, "To the church of God that is Corinth, to those who are sanctified in Christ Jesus, called to be saints" (1 Cor. 1:2; see also 2 Cor. 1:1; Phil. 1:1; Col. 1:2). Here is a reminder that our joining the church is not merely a matter of our choice to do so or of picking a particular church from among the various possibilities in our community. Each of us is called and made holy, sanctified, in Christ. God has acted, and we have responded. Because we have been made holy in Christ, we are called saints, literally, the holy ones.

In understanding ourselves as members of the community of saints, the corporate and the individual meanings of our incorporation into the Christian covenant community are brought together. The mission and ministry of the church are carried out through the ministry of each of its members, persons who display a vast diversity of gifts of age, gender, race, nationality, place, status, talent and skill, suffering, and education. The individual Christian is never alone in ministry, for always it is the ministry of the community which she or he brings to that place.

FULFILL YOUR MINISTRY

An important step in building community is to encourage people to see how their Christian covenant is linked to their daily lives. In what ways are the issues, decisions, and challenges that Christians face in their daily lives related to the commitments they have made in their baptism? Through the waters of baptism we emerge into a new life, rooted in the life, death, and resurrection of Jesus Christ. Therefore, ministry is a new way of being, not just a way of doing. We do not choose to become "lay ministers." In our baptism we have been made ministers. The words Paul wrote to Archippus—"See that you fulfill the ministry which you have received in the Lord" (Col. 4:17 [RSV, 1952])—are as applicable to Christians today as they were to him.

Christians are engaged in ministry all over God's world. This ministry takes place:

- wherever a Christian happens to be;
- whenever a Christian is called to minister;
- with whomever a Christian happens to meet;
- using whatever gifts a Christian has been given.

The range of possibilities for ministry is so extensive and open-ended that Christians need help in focusing on ways they can most effectively use their gifts of time, talent, energy, and situations in ministry. Saying yes also means that one must learn how to say no to a demand without feeling guilty. Ministry involves both focusing on priorities and letting go. Early in Jesus' ministry crowds began to flock to him with their sick and demon-possessed family members and friends. He cured many during the day. Early the next morning he went out by himself to a deserted place to pray. His disciples went to him saying, "Everyone is searching for you." His fame as a healer had spread far. He knew how much all these people needed his help. But Jesus said to them, "Let us go on to the neighboring towns, so that I may proclaim the message there also; for that is what I came out to do" (Mark 1:38). Speaking and living the good news were his priorities.

As Christians grow in their awareness of the significance of their baptismal commitments in their daily lives, it becomes increasingly important that the baptizing community explore how it might be more effective in preparing, supporting, and challenging the members in their ministry.

Church leaders need to ask whether or not they are providing times and places for strengthening the spirit of the *laos* (see chapter 6). The congregation's teachers are responsible for members knowing the good news of God in Christ and practicing how to proclaim that by work and example in schools, in homes, in offices, on the streets, and in voting booths (see chapter 5). Each group in the congregation needs to ask if it is a setting in which the members can experience reconciliation and respect and seeking Christ in each member. The church needs to be the place where we learn how to live the Christian way so that we can be co-creators of God's family wherever we go (see chapter 4).

The twelve men whom Jesus called to accompany him were both disciples and apostles. Disciples are pupils. Apostles are those who are sent. These twelve lived with Jesus, learning how to follow him. Then he sent them out to do what they had learned from him. There were others, such as Mary and Martha and Paul, who also were taught and sent. And today the baptizing community is discipled and sent.

The breakthrough to ministering with power comes with the reformation of our understanding and practice of ministering with the community of God's covenanted people.

2

Biblical Models of Ministry

Because we are a visual people, increasingly so in this age of television, pictures, stories, metaphors, and models give us ideas and values for living. In this we are amazingly close to the people of pre-Gutenberg times, whose ideas and values were shaped by stained-glass windows, stories, symbols, and signs.

However, we know that the pictures of "ministry" and "mission" and "church" that most of us carry now are not as accurate or liberating or full of the power we need in order to be God's people today and tomorrow.

How do we find and create and use the pictures—the stories, symbols, signs, and images—that can engage and strengthen the people of God?

THE BIBLE AS THE FAMILY STORYBOOK

Some of the pictures from our family storybook, the Bible, come in the form of stories and chronicles. Others come in genealogies and poetry. William R. White, in *Speaking in Stories*, has said, "Unless we learn to know the stories and events, the dreams and aspirations, the promises and pledges that shaped our biblical ancestors, how shall we grow into our baptism as members of the family of God?"[1]

Other pictures come from the stories and histories of persons and movements that carried the good news of Jesus Christ through two thousand years and around the earth. The next chapter will call attention to some of these pictures and the way in which they inform the ministry of today.

It is not enough just to note that the Bible is a source of pictures that can give power for ministry. The process of finding and using these stories requires at least the following elements to link the lives of the people of the stories to people today and to give them power for their ministry now.

Recognition of the Nature of the Bible

First, too many Christians believe that the Bible was written by "one or two" persons, put between two covers, and handed down from generation to generation. While such a statement may be a caricature of our understanding of the process, the general thrust of it is all too accurate. If we are to know the stories of our biblical ancestors well enough to empower the people of God in ministry today, we must forge links between the material on the page and the material in people's lives.

Probably the most critical assumption we need to help each other make is that the writers of the Bible were trying to be faithful ministers of God by handing down their understandings to their children and their children's children.

These stories are alive on many different levels:

- They are the stories of the original persons to whom the events happened.
- They became the stories of those who told them later on, and of those who wrote them down.
- They become our stories, and we tell them to understand and support who we are and to shape what our descendants shall be.

For all these people in their different times and places, God's story became their story.

We can enhance our appreciation of the stories in the Bible by imagining the other events that happened or the stories that were told and not written down, those that were not included in the biblical canon. For example, where was Sarah when Abraham took Isaac up the mountain for the sacrifice? What happened to Zebedee and the hired servants when James and John left them to follow Jesus? We need to learn to read between the lines to reach a more accurate and fuller understanding.

We need to celebrate all the different forms in which stories and histories in the Bible are told—through psalms and music, poetry, short stories, drama, genealogies, wise sayings, prophetic utterances, gospels, letters, and apocalyptic visions.

Affirmation of the Authority
of All Christian People

A second essential element in linking the biblical stories to our story is the affirmation of the authority and responsibility of all Christians to "dig around" in the Bible and other historical materials, and to tell and listen to each other's stories.

In one New Testament sermon the newly baptized were told, "Always be ready to make your defense to anyone who demands from you an accounting for the hope that is in you" (1 Peter 3:15). They needed to know how to be "a royal priesthood, a holy nation," how to be used as "God's own people in order that you may proclaim the mighty acts of him who called you out of darkness into his marvelous light" (1 Peter 2:9 [RSV]).

As members of the community of faith, all of us are responsible for living out our baptismal vows. To do so we must know what the faith is and how to confess it. As people who know we have been given new life in Christ, we need to learn how to recognize and tell others the ways in which God is giving new life for persons and groups and institutions around us. Though the responsibility belongs to each of us, this knowing and learning become fulfilled only as we help each other in living as members of Christ's priesthood.

Our baptism gives us the authority and permission to find out through the many avenues available to us what God is calling us to do. For too long laity have expected the clergy and others with formal theological education to define the Christian life for them by teaching or by example. If we, as the people of God, are to create pictures with power, we need to know that we have both the right and the responsibility to ask questions, pull the materials apart, and analyze them. We can explore the ways in which God is acting in a variety of revelations today, some of which may break through our traditional interpretation of "Christian."

Imagination to Put Ourselves into the Story

A third essential element in linking the biblical stories to our stories is the imagination to put ourselves into the stories and pictures of others, both those of our time and place and those other times and places.

Imagination does not just happen; imagination needs creating and nurturing and practicing. Blocks have to be removed in order for it to flower.

One block is the assumption there are only right and wrong answers and that those with special theological education always have the right answers. Related to this block is the fear of failing, of appearing to be an uneducated or stupid person. We can chip away at this block by asking questions that do not have specific answers and then encouraging others to respond. Noting carefully the words each person uses is an important way to affirm the gifts and values of each. Many of the questions we face today show us the ambiguity in much of our knowledge of the world, and we need the different perspectives of each of us to approach the wholeness of the truth. Planning time for people to meet in small groups is important, so that each person is given the opportunity to be heard. Rather than pursuing the "right" answer, we may do better to see how many different solutions we can find to the questions we face.

A second block to the blossoming of imagination is the ease with which we obtain some answers in our world. Seemingly complex problems are solved by "instant" answers in a half-hour television show. To take advantage of computer scoring, more and more examinations are designed to be answered by yes or no, 1 or 0. We turn to the experts, the persons with big names and charisma, to find the answers rather than working out some of the possibilities for ourselves. Probably one of the most important responsibilities of the Christian community today is to support one another in trying out ways to nurture imagination.

Doing so would help to remove a third block—lack of practice. Without practice our minds become brittle, tight, inflexible. One form of practice would be to allow time at regular meetings for persons to tell some of their stories. The question "What one thing about you at this time is important for the group to know?" might be used to prompt the stories.

Another form of practice is to ask a group, after it has defined a purpose or goal, to list several different ways that that purpose or goal might be reached. Premature closure on decisions reinforces our readiness to assume only one right answer.

Probably the most formidable block to imagination is the fear of change. We do not want to imagine ourselves walking in another's footsteps, because then we would have to change our definition of the other person and of ourselves. We do not want to imagine new pictures with power for today, because, if they truly carry power, they will move us to act in new ways, to give up our comfortable ruts, and to walk unmarked paths.

The creation, nurture, and practice of imagination is both the responsibility and gift of the Christian community, the community of friends who can be open to each other because they know that whatever happens, they have come from God and they are with God forever.

SOME BIBLE PICTURES

There are many stories of ministry in the Bible. Some of them are particularly powerful in giving vision and strength to our ministries. Through considering a few of these stories here, you will gain some ideas about how to use biblical material to strengthen laity in ministry.

Old Testament Stories

We will begin with some stories from the Old Testament about Abraham, the kings and prophets, and the community builders.

Abraham, the faithful friend of God. "The friend of God" is how James, the pastor and church builder, described Abraham in the epistle he wrote about building the church community in the first century of the Christian era (James 2:23). Over six hundred years before, the prophet Isaiah had also called Abraham the "friend" of God (Isa. 41:8). The story of God and Abraham is a story of friendship, the story of two "persons" whose relationship and response to each other present a powerful model for our relationship with God and with each other. This story has strengthened the people of God from the early days of the Old Testament right up to our own time.

From the beginning of their relationship with God, the Hebrew people had known God to be the God of Abraham. This identification was evident when God addressed Moses at the burning bush (Ex. 3:15). The deacon Stephen, in the sermon he preached before his stoning, told the people that in rejecting Jesus they were rejecting the God of Abraham (Acts 7:2).

When we read the story of Abraham in Genesis 12 to 25:11, we are taken back to distant times. Probably the story was told around campfires with bits handed down by different groups until gradually it was shaped into the epic of one man, his family, and God.

The story of God and Abraham indicates three unique qualities of God's personality. First, this God calls people out of their accustomed places and keeps calling them, even when they continue to be aliens and strangers. Second, the God of Abraham is one who makes promises and keeps them even when they seem impossible. Third, Abraham found out that this God demands each person be prepared to sacrifice the very best that has been given to him or her so that the "friends of God" will depend on God alone. Whenever we remember God as the God of Abraham, we are re-called to this God.

We are also reminded of how Abraham responded to God. Abraham was willing to move when God called. All along he let God make the changes; he was always ready to go to the new place to which God called him. Abraham trusted in God's promises; he trusted so much that he even convinced God to continue to take care of the people of Sidon so that God could continue to keep the promise to love. Abraham walked with his friend God through the valley of the shadow of death to the place for the sacrifice of Isaac when God's promise and Abraham's trust were on the line. Many years later the God of Abraham walked with God's only Son, Jesus, to the cross outside Jerusalem. The God of Abraham was with Stephen and with the early Christians in the difficult first-century environment of Jerusalem.

The saga of Abraham's faithful friendship with God has supported ministry over the centuries. It provides a model for ministry today.

The kingdom of priests and a holy nation. When Moses received the Ten Commandments from God on Mount Sinai, God gave him this message for the people: "You have seen what I did to the Egyptians, and how I bore you on eagles' wings and brought you to myself. Now therefore, if you obey my voice and keep my covenant, you shall be my treasured possession out of all the peoples. Indeed, the whole earth is mine, but you shall be for me a priestly kingdom and a holy nation" (Ex. 19:4-6).

The covenant between God and the people of Israel became the core of their identity. God had delivered them from slavery in Egypt and would care for them. They, in turn, would be obedient to God. However, often they did not follow God's voice, and they did not want to be burdened with the responsibilities of being God's particular people. Throughout the Old Testament we find the retelling of this story and the recommitment of the people to the covenant. Much of Deuteronomy is a retelling of the story by the priests in forms to be used in worship (see, for example, Deut. 6:20-25; 7:6-11). The Hebrew hymnbook, the Psalms, contains the hymns they sang that reminded them of who they were as a covenant people.

Just as God's deliverance of the Israelites out of Egypt made possible the covenant between God and these particular people, the deliverance of all people from sin and death through Christ made possible a new covenant and a new community of God's people.

When the writer of 1 Peter described the church as the people of God, the Greek word he used for people was *laos*, the source of our word *laity*. Too often we think of the laity as a lower form of Christian, compared to those who are the "real" ministers.[2] According to the Bible, all are part of the people, the *laos*, of God. Conversely, to be the people of God is to be selected by God for a particular purpose.

The picture of the royal priesthood captured Martin Luther's imagination. He saw the whole gathering of Christians as a priesthood, bringing the whole world to God to be made holy. It is this picture that is brought to life in the welcome the congregation gives to those who are newly baptized in the service of Holy Baptism in the *Book of Common Prayer* and quoted in chapter 1 (p. 16).

These pictures of a royal priesthood and holy nation are very powerful for good or ill. Too often the dream of the church governing a people has led to destructive consequences, as in the Middle Ages or in the Massachusetts Bay Colony. The idea of a nation as "a holy nation" too often is the cover for colonization, aggrandizement, and oppression of others. However, this concept also offers new insight into the importance of the church as the body of Christ. The whole church, not just individual Christians, is called to be used by God to build the reign of justice and peace among all people. The witness of the church was an important factor in the liberation of East Germany, and the church continues to be in the center of the struggle against apartheid in South Africa.

Throughout the history of the Hebrew people two roles were crucial for Israel's calling to be a holy nation. One was the vocation of leader or ruler, the other the vocation of prophet, the person who spoke on behalf of God. Always it was clear that both were being used as God's ministers. Ahab was a king in the holy nation of Israel, but Elijah had to remind him that in that nation the king was subject to the same law of God as were the common people (1 Kings 18:17-18). Throughout Israel's history, the kings had to be reminded of this special calling for all the nation to be God's people. Also prophets vividly expanded the people's understanding of God's plan for the nation by pointing to rulers who were created for God's purposes even when they did not recognize the God of Israel. Isaiah said that the Lord had called Cyrus, the ruler of Persia, his "shepherd," and said that he would carry out God's purpose (Isa. 44:28). Cyrus, who did "not know [God]" (Isa. 45:4), was used by God to defeat Babylonia, making possible the return of the exiles to Jerusalem (see Ezra 1:1-4). Several hundred years after Cyrus, Ezra praised God, who put into the heart of Cyrus's successor, Artaxerxes, "to glorify the house of the Lord in Jerusalem" (Ezra 7:27).

Many different roles were needed for the people of Israel to fulfill their special calling for all the nation to be God's holy people, a model of justice and righteousness in the world. Today each Christian has to ask, "How does God want to use me in this time and in this place?" Each Christian community has to search to discern God's purpose for it in the place it now is with the members it now has. Both persons and communities who speak on behalf of God today are called further to become aware of those persons and events in the world through whom God is fulfilling God's plan for justice and righteousness today.

Community builders. When the people of Israel returned to Jerusalem from their exile in Babylon, much needed to be done to reestablish themselves in a working and worshiping community. Ezra and Nehemiah had the very practical tasks of rebuilding the walls, taking a census of the people, and shaping the pattern of life and worship in Jerusalem. Ezra led in the rebuilding of the temple, and all the people helped—the masons and carpenters (Ezra 3:7), the herdsmen who raised animals for sacrifice (6:17), as well as the Levites who staffed the temple (7:24).

Nehemiah kept excellent records of the people who helped rebuild the city—priests, goldsmiths, perfumers, temple servants, merchants, and many others, women as well as men, whose contributions are acknowledged in Nehemiah 3:1-32.

Other historians carried on the important work of writing the history of the people. First and Second Chronicles helped the people know their roots so they might understand who they were and have a vision for their future. Sages and scribes used proverbs and philosophical sayings, found in Proverbs, Ecclesiastes, and Job, to explore the meaning of God's continuing creation and revelation. Others wrote hymns, and some edited and collected old and new hymns in the Book of Psalms. Each of these people used unique gifts—musical, intellectual, editorial, administrative, artistic, mechanical, and visionary—for strengthening the people of God. Their work shaped the culture and environment of their time and place and of the times to come, even the time of Jesus.

Throughout the centuries since then there have been many, many persons and communities whose response to God's call to be the "holy nation" has reflected the diversity of the gifts of talents and cultures and opportunities they have been given.

At the time of Ezra and Nehemiah there was no separation of church and state, sacred and secular. Today the situation is very different, and we have to rethink the way in which the story of God's action in their lives may be true also for our situation. One place where the Christian community is very conscious of its call to build the nation is the People's Republic of China. Christian men and women, intellectuals, workers and farmers, lay and ordained, rural and urban people, all understand their Christian vocation to contribute to fullness of life for all in China.

Jesus' Ministry

There are many different ways to look at the Gospel pictures of Jesus' ministry that can empower Christians for their day-to-day ministry. When we read through a Gospel all at one time, we are confronted by the total effect of the person and presence of Jesus.

Or we can choose a theme of Jesus' ministry, such as that with outsiders and outcasts, or look at ways in which Jesus received ministry from others. Examining stories that tell us how Jesus ministered to the outcasts and welcomed outsiders guides us in our own ministries.

A description of Jesus' acts as given in Mark 1:14-39 can expand our vision of the possibilities of the deeds he expects of us today. In Luke 4:16-19, the story of Jesus reading from the prophet Isaiah in the synagogue at Nazareth outlines the ministry he would bring in Palestine and would also commit to us.

Over the centuries since Jesus was born, lived, died, and rose again, his followers have tried in different ways to do his work. Martyrs, desert mothers and fathers, and theologians have all been understood to be doing Jesus' work. In the New Testament Peter and Paul give us two quite different pictures of ministry.

Much of what Jesus did consisted of simple acts of walking, touching, telling God's story in the ordinary locales of daily life—home, church, and street. Always his ministry was responsive to the needs the people brought to him, and always it was for the sole purpose of telling the people that God's power to bring abundant life was at hand.

Sometimes it is very helpful to look at the stories of the followers of Jesus in other places and cultures to stretch our imaginations about ways in which we might live Jesus' ministry. *The Gospel in Solentiname* is a collection of stories of Jesus told by lay people in a Nicaraguan context.[3] Songs from Africa and from China, novels such as *Silence* by Shisaku Endo of Japan,[4] paintings by Indian Christians—all of these can give us new directions and pose new questions for the followers of Jesus today.

Witnesses of the Resurrection

Early on the Sunday morning following Jesus' death on the cross, his friends went to the tomb where he was buried to finish the burial rites. But his body was gone. The soldiers who had been sent by the authorities to guard the tomb reported that his body had disappeared. Officials paid the guards to say that Jesus' disciples had stolen his body (Matt. 28:11-15).

Jesus' women followers were the first to know the truth that God had brought Jesus through death to new life. An angel gave them this astounding news at the tomb that morning. Jesus himself met Mary Magdalene in the garden and told her the good news (John 20:11-18). Slowly the disciples came to believe it, for they experienced Jesus' strong presence with them. Then they understood much of what he had said and done while he was with them before the crucifixion.

Now the disciples knew their task was to be witnesses of his resurrection. They all risked their lives to tell this good news wherever they could. Peter and John and the other disciples became bolder than they had ever thought possible and preached Jesus' resurrection even to the hostile rulers and scribes of Jerusalem. Stephen was stoned to death for proclaiming the power of Jesus to make all things new. Paul met the risen Christ on the road to Damascus and was turned around to a new life as a witness of Jesus' resurrection to the Gentile world.

Paul's letters, especially those to the Corinthians and to the Galatians, show us how the calling to be resurrection people created unique perspectives for dealing with the problems of becoming a faithful community. Baptism was the drama of going into the waters of death and coming out into a new life. Breaking bread together was an occasion at which the risen Christ came to take part in the life of his disciples. Through confession and forgiveness, persons found reconciliation and community. These practices offered a way for Christians to be restored to a new relationship with God through the risen Christ over and over.

A Christian has always been and is today, by definition, a person who is part of the resurrection community and witness to God's power to bring life out of death. All ministry always has been and still is centered in witnessing to God's ministry of resurrection.

The early Christian community was composed of two groups.[5] One was made up of wandering charismatic figures who believed they were followers of Jesus the prophet (see Luke 9:23-27, 57-62; 10:1-11; 12:22-31); other Lukan passages, as well as similar ones in Matthew and Mark, tell us about the beliefs and practices of these people. They were understood to be "apostles." The other group consisted of the people in settled communities throughout Asia Minor. Luke-Acts especially tells us much about these communities. The writer, Luke, was a pastoral theologian who wanted the settled communities to see themselves in "partnership with the wandering prophets."[6] The Gospels of Matthew and Mark also reflect the interests and needs of those two groups in the early church, the people for whom they wrote their Gospels.

Luke showed that there are many different ways to respond to Jesus' call. The whole church was to be missionary—both those who wandered and those who lived in settled communities. God uses the whole church "to turn the world upside down" (see Acts 17:6).

Throughout the history of the church there have been many different responses to Jesus' call and many different ways in which the church has fulfilled its missionary task. Because of these differences there has always been controversy over who was to be understood as authentic Christians— clergy or laity; those in monastic orders or those without; evangelists or social activists.

In Luke-Acts, the author introduces not only Paul, Peter, and the other apostles, but also many laypersons:

- Ananias, host to Paul in Damascus (9:10-22)
- Barnabas, landowner, then missionary (4:36; 9:27)
- Cornelius, Roman centurion (10:1-33)
- Lydia, seller of dyes and head of household (16:14-15)
- Priscilla and Aquila, tentmakers (18:2-3)

The letters of Paul and his associates also bear witness to the contributions made to the early church by various people who were not included in the "official" leadership of the church. In Romans 16, Paul mentions Phoebe, a businesswoman in Rome, and many others, including Andronicus and Junia, Paul's companions in prison in Rome. Others are mentioned in the other epistles, for example, Zenas, a lawyer, in Titus 3:13; and Onesimus, the runaway slave, and his owner, Philemon.

As we become involved in these Bible stories and bring our own stories to them, we will be following the biblical writers who have gone before. For this is the way some of the Bible was written and has been transmitted to us across the generations and cultures.

The faithfulness of our ministry is grounded in the context of these stories. Our specific ministry is a part of the whole story of God's people. We have the responsibility of making available to the people of God these resources that give lasting meaning to their ministries.

3

The People of God in History

For many Christians "church" is where we go on Sundays; ministers are the people who are the leaders; the church speaks when church leaders make pronouncements or take stands. Laity are those who "pray and pay" on Sundays but mostly live in the world and see little connection between that and their church experience.

Such assumptions have been fostered by the pictures of reality the church has presented in its theology, its history, its structures, its models of authentic Christian life, and its spirituality.

Therefore, if we are going to turn the church around to become what it is called to be—the people of God, each of whom is to be engaged in God's ministry—then we have to change the picture of the church that is the ground of our thinking and practice.

History is a way of understanding reality, and it is always presented within the perspective of the people who compose history. Therefore, any historical presentation is limited by the perspectives of those who have written it. Expanding our understanding of reality necessitates exploration of the history of those who are not part of the establishment traditions.

The process of recouping the history of women has been powerful for both men and women. It has given women the power of identity. By shaping a new perspective on the past, it has given women power in the present to break out of the "expected," to shape different futures. It continues to bring to light stories that challenge women and give them models to help them move toward fullness of life. Likewise, the process of opening up black history, revising African history from the perspective of Africans, doing Native American studies, or revising Asian history from the purview of Asians has given each of these peoples clearer perception of who they are and determination to be all they can be. Such viewing of history from the "other side" or the "underside" is not always accepted, for it confronts the customary and comfortable story of those who have maintained it. Still, if and when the traditionalists are ready to be open to the other story, people now and in the future will be given new resources for moving toward fullness of life. So it has happened for men who have brought women's story into reality and for whites who have listened to and been made more whole by owning black history as part of their own story.

The deliberate work of opening up the history of the church from the perspective of the laity still needs to be done. The only book specifically directed toward this task was *The Layman in Christian History*, edited by Stephen Charles Neill (a bishop) and Hans-Ruedi Weber (a layman), published in 1963 and long out of print.[1] Other books contain chapters about laity, such as "The Practice of Christian Life: The Birth of the Laity," in *Christian Spirituality*, edited by Bernard McGinn, John Meyendorff, and Jean Leclerq.[2] New studies in biblical and Christian history as different as Wayne Meeks's *The First Urban Christians* and Elizabeth Schüssler Fiorenza's *In Memory of Her*[3] have unearthed material that tells the story of the early church from the perspective of the laity.

In this chapter we will look at several periods in church history from the perspective of the laity rather than from that of the popes, bishops, and theologians. Seeing the church from a different perspective may give us power to undertake the ministry of all the people of God. In each period we will ask: "What does being a faithful layperson look like? What is authentic Christian living?" History can become a strengthening process for laypersons only as they engage in it themselves. To change the picture of the church from that which is the property and responsibility of a few to that which is the property and responsibility of all the people of God requires much work and practice. Every part of the congregation's program—its worship, education, and community life—needs to involve Christians in learning the stories of those who have gone before and using them to give life and power to our ministry today.

THE EARLY CHURCH

The Christian church started as a lay movement. As long as the church was seen primarily as the fellowship of the Holy Spirit, the laity took an active part in its organization and liturgy. We have already seen in the last chapter how the New Testament recognizes the role of laypersons in response to the ministry of Jesus and in the founding of the church. Several passages from writings in the first centuries of the church give us pictures of the life of these early Christians. One such passage is in a letter written by Diogenetus, a Christian, to an inquiring friend in the second or third century of the Christian era:

> Though they live in Greek and barbaric cities, as each man's lot is cast, and follow the local customs in dress and food and the rest of their living, their own way of life which they display is wonderful and admittedly strange. They live in their native lands like foreigners, they take part in everything like citizens, and endure everything like aliens. Every foreign land is their native land, and every native land like a foreign country. Like everyone else they marry, they have children, but they do not expose their infants. They set a common table but not a common bed. They find themselves in flesh, but they do not live after the flesh. They pass their days on earth, but they are citizens of heaven. They obey the prescribed laws, and at the same time surpass the laws by their lives.[4]

From the beginning of the church Christian people had undertaken the *ministry of service* to others. In Acts we are told about how they shared their goods (4:32—5:11) and collected money to assist Christians in need (11:29-30). Tertullian, a layman, perhaps a lawyer, who lived from about A.D. 160 to 225 tells us they had a kind of money chest

> to pay for the nourishment and burial of the poor, to support boys and girls who are orphan or destitute; and old people who are confined to the house; and those who have been shipwrecked; and any who are in the mines or banished to islands, or in prison, or are pensioners because of their confession, provided they are suffering because they belong to the followers of God.[5]

Also, from the early days Christian people took responsibility for telling the good news of Jesus Christ and for teaching the faith and practice of their Way (see Acts 9:2). The Book of Acts and the letters of Paul have many references to the preaching and teaching that was done in the churches of the time. Two of the outstanding teachers in the early church were laymen. One was Justin Martyr who lived from about A.D. 100 to

165. He taught for a time in Ephesus and then opened a Christian school in Rome and wrote several papers in which he worked out a rational defense of the Christian faith. He was beheaded because of his faith.

About twenty years later Origen was born in a Christian family in Alexandria. As an adult, he was appointed by the bishop of Alexandria to be head of the catechetical school. About twelve years later he fled to Palestine because of trouble in Alexandria. The bishops there would not let him preach as a layman, so he returned to Alexandria. In A.D. 230 he returned to Palestine and was ordained. His bishop in Alexandria was so angered by this that he took away his post in the school, deposed him as priest, and exiled him. Origen went to Caesarea and opened another school. He wrote many books on doctrine, the Bible, and prayer. At the end of his life he was tortured and imprisoned.

In this period martyrdom was a common experience for committed Christians. There were intermittent persecutions such as that by Nero in A.D. 64, in which he made the Christians scapegoats for the fire of Rome. In 250 Emperor Decius ordered that all who would not sacrifice to the state gods should die. After his death there was a pause in persecution until 303 when Emperor Diocletian ordered all churches and Bibles burned. In 304 he gave orders to kill Christians. It was only with Constantine's victory over the old regime in 313 that the persecutions were stopped, religious toleration proclaimed, and the Christian church given legal status.

During these first centuries, both clergy and laity were imprisoned, tortured, and put to death. Perpetua, a mother from Carthage in North Africa, was put to death about A.D. 203. Alban, a Briton who gave his life in place of the priest whom he had sheltered and who had converted and baptized him, was executed about 305. Maximilian, the son of a Roman soldier, was executed in about 295 because he refused to serve in the Roman army.

THE CHURCH IN THE MIDDLE AGES

After Constantine gave legal status to the Christian church, its organizational structure grew more complex. The division between clergy and laity and between the church and the world grew more pronounced. As the hierarchy increased its responsibility for the ministries of preaching, teaching, pastoring, and worship, the people increasingly were expected only to pray and pay for the maintenance of the church. By the twelfth century the canon lawyer Gratian wrote the logical conclusion in his

Decretals: "There are two kinds of Christians, the clergy who are to be devoted to divine office and contemplation and to rule themselves, . . . and the other sort of Christians who are called 'lay folk.' "[6]

For several hundred years, beginning in the third century, some Christians sought to make a total commitment to God by going into the desert or some other solitary place to live as hermits. In time, some of them formed orders of monks and much later of nuns. Benedict of Nursia, a layman in the sixth century, formed a community of other committed laymen to live by a rule that balanced prayer, study, and manual labor. This rule was the foundation of the Benedictine Order.

Later the layman Francis of Assisi created a community of laymen to wander through the countryside preaching and teaching. The hierarchy was alarmed by teaching done by laypersons not in its control. It forced Francis to be ordained a deacon and eventually required all Franciscan monks to be priests, because at the time priests were among the few to be educated.

One of the best-known people in this period of church history is Augustine. His theology laid the groundwork for scholars right up to our own day. However, as a young man he was more noted for his dissolute life. He dabbled in many different philosophies as well as following his lust. However, in time, the influence and prayers of his mother, Monica, a devout Christian laywoman, along with other factors, led to his conversion and the subsequent contributions he made to the Christian church. Without Monica's strong and persistent faith, all that Augustine brought to the church might have been lost.

Great cathedrals stand today as monuments to the firm faith of the people in the Middle Ages. The soaring vaults and beautiful stonework bear witness to the majesty of God and the beauty of holiness. The building of cathedrals was made possible only by the work of masons, carpenters, artisans, water haulers, weavers, glass makers, and others, many of whom were lay Christians. People in the town and region shared their gifts and abilities.

Some kings and rulers in this period were Christian. For example, Alfred the Great, King of Wessex (A.D. 849-99), is remembered for leading his army in the successful defense of Christian England against the pagan Danes. He also led an important reform of the church's structure so it could do God's mission better, and he led a revival of learning among his people.

THE REFORMATION:
RAISED EXPECTATIONS FOR LAITY

The movement for reform of the church broke out during a dynamic time for the church and world. In the eleventh to the thirteenth centuries, the Crusades were mounted to wrest from Islam the control of Jerusalem and the surrounding lands made holy by the life of Jesus. Although this main purpose of the Crusades was not accomplished, this movement, which involved vast resources of lay people and money from Europe, had a profound effect on the whole culture, religious and secular. The organization of these great enterprises led to a breakdown of the medieval feudal system and supported the growth of towns and cities. The experience of the Crusades fueled desires to explore and control new worlds, material worlds rather than spiritual.

Following widespread illiteracy in the Middle Ages, there was a growing desire for education, which was first answered by the monastic movement and then by both lay teaching missionaries and by universities.

The increased literacy of the laity was accompanied by the new art of printing, by the encouragement of the use of local languages given by the writings of Dante and Chaucer, and by the translation of the Bible into German by Martin Luther and into English by Tyndale and Coverdale. A sixteenth-century chronicler reflected on the impact of the laity reading the Bible:

> The gospel that Christ gave to the clergy and doctors . . . has become vulgar and more open to laymen and women who can read than it usually is to quite learned clergy of good intelligence. And so the pearl of the gospel is scattered abroad and trodden underfoot by swine.[7]

John Wycliffe's followers in England, known as the Lollards, based their faith on the Bible and personal faith. This movement, which was strongest in the fifteenth century, gave laity a way to speak articulately for reform in the church. In particular they denounced an overbearing priesthood and misuse of the endowments of the church, and called for a return to primitive simplicity and morality. Although this movement declined, it was a forerunner of the Reformation, which followed in the sixteenth century.

The reformers of the sixteenth century—Ulrich Zwingli (1484-1521), Martin Luther (1483-1546), John Calvin (1509-64), and John Knox (c. 1513-72)—attracted followers because they preached in a rapidly changing political and social environment in which laity were demanding a voice in both the political and spiritual arenas. Conflicts were inevitable. Martin Luther first ignored, then preached against the peasants' revolt in Germany, blaming the princes and lords for their godless exploitation and calling for repentance on all sides because the gospel's claims cannot be instituted by violence. In England the reformers supported Henry VIII's nationalization of the church by the state. However, soon it was obvious that replacing the pope by the king would not necessarily bring the longed-for reform of religion. Sir Thomas More (1487-1535) was chancellor of England and accepted the full responsibility of being a Christian within the difficult and complex political situation of the time.

> Martin Luther wrote regarding the priesthood of believers: all we who believe on Christ are kings and priests in Christ. . . . Christ has obtained for us this favor, if we believe in Him: that just as we are His brethren and co-heirs and fellow kings with Him, so we should be also fellow-priests with Him, and venture with confidence, through the spirit of faith, to come unto the presence of God and cry "Abba, Father!" and to pray for one another, and to do all things which we see done and figured in the visible and corporeal office of priesthood.[8]

There were a number of effects of the Reformation that might have restored the laity as the royal priesthood. Most important was the avail-ability of the Bible to the people in their own language. Provision for the education of all people expanded rapidly, and lay people were given a large share of responsibility for this. Catechisms and collections of family prayers were prepared for the use of heads of households.

In England lay people were appointed as teachers in congregations or for whole cities. Increased participation of the laity in worship encouraged congregational music, and the Psalms were set to music for congregational singing. Both the bread and the wine were now distributed to the laity in the Eucharist. Also, in the Protestant churches, the laity were given control over the clergy through the new right to depose a preacher and call another.

In the Roman Catholic Church, the laity took an active part in the first part of the Council of Trent (1545-47), under the leadership of Pope Paul III. Laity were appointed by cardinals to be agents of reform. Plans were made for liturgical reforms and for catechisms to be used by laity in teaching. However, the next two meetings of the Council in 1551-52 and 1562-63 were consumed with defending the Roman Catholic Church against the Protestant movements, and the opportunities for laity in that church grew more and more limited. One area in which Catholic laity were encouraged was the arts. Painters and sculptors such as Michelangelo and Titian were commissioned to adorn Catholic buildings and portray the church's councils. Musicians such as Palestrina composed masses and motets.

Johann Sebastian Bach, who lived from 1685 to 1750, was a singer and choir director in Leipzig at the time when the Protestant churches were growing stronger. He wrote his music to be used in the worship of these churches. It has continued to give strength to the spirits of women and men in the whole world ever since.

The church owes much to the men and women who have used their gifts to design church buildings that serve as gathering places for the Christian family and as signs of God's presence. William of Sens was a twelfth-century architect for the reconstruction of Canterbury Cathedral after a fire. Christopher Wren, 1632-1723, was both an architect and professor of Astronomy at Oxford. After the Great Fire of London in 1666, he was given the commission to design the rebuilding of the city with St. Paul's Cathedral as its focal point.

The sixteenth century through the first half of the seventeenth century was an exciting and a frantic time. The religious issues of the time cannot be separated from the political power struggles between states and power blocs within states, the commercial revolution, and changing class structures. It was a time of religious wars and persecutions, both Catholic and Protestant. The vocation of many lay Christians came to be martyrdom.

In some ways the movement for reform accomplished little. The Augsburg Confession, written by Lutheran nobles, all laymen, insisted that the true church was the place were "the word is rightly preached and the sacraments properly administered." This required an educated, professional clergy who quickly became more important than the laity. Laywomen were leaders in the public life of the Separatist movement in England. While laymen held the public positions, the responsibility for teaching, for spiritual formation, and for works of charity was given to the women to be done privately in and through the homes.[9]

The vitality that produced the imaginative work of Galileo, the astronomer and mathematician (1564-1642) who confirmed Copernicus's finding of a hundred years earlier that the sun was the center of the universe, was diminished when the Roman Catholic Church forced Galileo to recant. Even so, Galileo's recantation had little long-term effect. Both his findings and his empirical method had already provided a radically different way of looking at the world.

THE CHURCH IN THE INDUSTRIAL REVOLUTION: LAITY SHAPE SOCIETY

In the eighteenth and nineteenth centuries, many of the patterns were formed that gave the people of God their work of ministry in the twentieth century. The nations of Europe were defined and strengthened. Some Christian laypersons understood that they had a particular responsibility to shape the state in a Christian way. Prince Bismarck, leader in Prussia and the German Empire from 1861 to 1890, believed that the kingdom of God could be built by ethical and social action.

The Industrial Revolution began in England in the last quarter of the eighteenth century and in Europe after 1815. Peasants moved from small agricultural villages into the cities, hoping to work in the new factories. This movement led to mass unemployment, large-scale child labor, illiteracy, and wretched living conditions under slum landlords.

The French Revolution, which began in 1789, fueled the movement toward criticism of all institutions—political, social, economic, and religious. The new patterns of thought and values by which people explored and measured the world led to increasing materialism and widespread religious dissatisfaction. In France the word *laic* had then and still has today a double significance: the layperson in the church and the person who violently rejects the church.

Yet there were Christian men and women throughout Europe who tried to be faithful to their calling to serve God. In England Christian middle-class persons took part in the reform movements of the mid-nineteenth century. For example, William Wilberforce (1759-1833) had wanted to be ordained, but his friends convinced him he could do more as a Christian in Parliament. There he pushed through the bill abolishing slavery.

Robert Raikes (1735-1811), the owner of the *Gloucester Journal* in England, started a Sunday school in 1780 to educate children who worked all week in the factories.

A wide variety of groups and organizations were developed within and alongside the traditional church structures to inspire, train, and support laity in their ministries. The Young Men's Christian Association was founded in 1844 and the Young Women's Christian Association in 1855. The Christian middle class put its money not only into industrial investment, but also into hospitals, schools, universities, urban relief agencies, and the establishment of the Christian churches worldwide. Christian laywomen played major roles as founders and financial backers of institutions and in missionary and service work at home and overseas.

Richard Rothe, a German layman, in his book *Christian Ethics* (1849), proclaimed that the work of Christianization of the world and building the kingdom was greater than the church alone could do and had to be done by lay people working in and through the state. He defined the task of clergy to be in the church teaching the faith and concluded, "Today we can no longer look for Christian saints within the Church."[10]

From the very beginning the followers of Jesus Christ have understood that they were commissioned to preach the gospel in all the world (Matt. 28:19). As the Christian church incorporated more members, it became inevitable that lay people—traders, soldiers, prisoners of war, and pilgrims—would spread the gospel wherever they went. Increasing nationalism and materialism led to the age of exploration. The Jesuit Order was founded in 1534, not only to combat the new Reformation movement, but also to do missionary work among the heathen. Most of the subsequent missionary work of the Roman Catholic Church has been done by the religious orders.

The missionary work of the Protestant churches expanded rapidly in the nineteenth century, and laypersons played a major part in this movement. Some were wives and children of ordained missionaries; others were teachers and agriculturists, doctors and nurses.

Still the most impressive Christian missionaries have been those who left their homeland to teach, heal, develop communities, or do business or government service. At the same time they witnessed through their faith and daily practice.

The preaching and teaching of the gospel in the worship and educational programs of the church worldwide have been critical in the struggle for liberation from all forms of oppression that have characterized the twentieth century. Marxist analysis and thought was considered helpful in some of these struggles because it appeared to offer ways to restore the pattern of life of the early church when "all who believed were together and had all things in common" (Acts 2:44). In China the present leaders of the Three Self Movement and the Christian Council of China were prepared for leadership in this changing nation by the Christian schools and colleges of pre-Communist China. The "base communities" in the liberation movement in Latin and South America are Bible study groups focused on freeing the laity to take responsibility for their own ministries in the redemption of society.

LAY LEADERSHIP IN THE UNITED STATES

Laity came to exercise significant control of the church in the Protestant colonies of North America because there were very few clergy. Many of the colonists had come precisely so that they might control their own practice of religion. The Catholic colonies maintained the traditional European pattern of control negotiated between the colonial governor and the church.

The frontier in actuality and in concept nurtured democratic ideas instead of hierarchical authority. Laymen became preachers or circuit riders in a form of Christian calling not seen before. However, increasing tension between the church's governing policies and the lay preachers' actual practice led to the curtailing of this activity by the institution.

In New Jersey many Anglican clergy closed the churches during the Revolution because they found it too painful to leave out the customary prayers for the English monarch. However, laypersons kept the churches open because they said it was necessary in that time of crisis to meet to pray together.

Laypersons who had found new freedom as Christians in their churches in the colonies were influential in providing for the separation of church and state in the Constitution of the United States. This concept has nurtured volunteerism and allowed any person or group, lay or ordained, to establish a free and indigenous religious body. Significantly, both those churches that have been founded in the United States, such as the Church of Christ and the Seventh Day Adventist Church, and those that have been restructured here, such as the Southern Baptists and American Methodists, strongly encourage lay leadership.

In the twentieth century, the church in the United States has grown primarily as an institution located in a building. Clergy have increasingly become professional specialists. More and more laypersons have been trained and employed as professional church workers, especially in the ministry of education. This increase was particularly marked in the Protestant churches between 1940 and 1970 and in the Roman Catholic Church since 1970. With this increasing professionalization of leadership has come the tendency for the rest of the laity to hand over power to the leadership, lay and ordained.

WHO ARE THE SAINTS?

Throughout its history, the Christian community has always remembered the lives of some of those who have been faithful followers of Jesus Christ. Many parts of the church have followed a calendar that guides the commemoration of these lives. This calendar is not static but changes (albeit slowly) as new persons are recognized as important for the church's remembrance. Sometimes these changes are made as the calendar is brought up to date. In the Pacific basin some churches celebrate the martyrdom of many Christians, lay and ordained, who gave their lives to save the lives of other Christians during World War II. Names are added to the calendar as the church is challenged to recognize the wideness of its fellowship. Recently the Anglican Church in New Zealand chose October 30 as a day on which to celebrate the holy women of the New Testament.

Nevertheless, the celebration of the lives of these "saints" has sometimes been a stumbling block to the full ministry of the people of God. We have mistakenly identified "saints" as extraordinary people who, in some way, seemed more than human. We tend to forget the biblical use of the word *saints* for ordinary people who are made God's special people in baptism. The church's calendar list of saints is a very narrow, limited list. Most people are on it because they were martyrs or bishops or theologians. However, the saints are all sorts of people using different gifts for their ministry in many different times and places.

Christians Using Different Gifts for Ministry

When we begin to list the names of Christians down through the centuries, we are amazed by the many different ways in which people have responded to God's call. There never has been only one right way to do God's ministry. In this book we can touch on only a few representative people.

Many of the leaders of newly independent nations of Africa have been Christian men and women educated in Christian schools; for example, Julius Nyerere in Tanzania, Kenneth Kaunda of Zambia, Robert Mugabe of Zimbabwe, and the late Oliver Tambo of the African National Congress in South Africa.

Early in 1990 there was a ground-breaking ceremony for the center of Samba-Likhaan: A Community of Artists in Manila in the Philippine Islands. During the ceremony these artists asked God to be present in their community so that:

> by this offering of all that we have, and all that
> we can do, and all that we are,
> we may render you due honor and thanks,
> and proclaim your wondrous goodness wholeheartedly.[11]

This community of artists has many exemplars throughout history and in our own time. Many of the great artists in history have been men and women who consciously used their great gifts of creativity to share with others the good news of Jesus Christ. Giotto, a painter of Florence in the late thirteenth century, and Sadao Watanabe, a Japanese painter and wood-cut artist in our own time, have both proclaimed the wonderful acts of God through their work.

Many Christian men and women have used their gifts of writing for God's mission. About A.D. 843 Dhuoda, wife of Bernard, son of a cousin of Charlemagne, wrote *Manual for My Son*, an explanation of the Christian life, for William, her sixteen-year-old son. In our own century, Flannery O'Conner was an American writer whose stories reflect her conviction of God's incarnation and reconciliation in all the world. Alan Paton used his gifts to tell the story of sin and brokenness and God's love in the tragedy of apartheid South Africa. Through his novels Shisaku Endo, a Roman Catholic author in Japan, is exploring the meaning of the gospel of Jesus Christ for the people of Japan and thus is expanding the meaning of Jesus Christ for all Christians.

Henry Gheon (1875-1944), a French playwright, founded a Christian theater. Both Dorothy Sayers and T. S. Eliot were twentieth-century Christian authors who wrote plays that examined the meaning of Christian faith and life.

After Gutenberg developed the process of using moveable type, the business of printing Bibles grew very rapidly. Christopher Plantin (c. 1520-89) lived in Antwerp, where he built up the largest European printing and publishing business of that day. Henry Buch, a master shoemaker in the seventeenth century, founded the "Shoemakers' Brotherhood" and later the "Tailors' Brotherhood" to support Christians in keeping their baptismal vows more perfectly in and through their crafts.

A servant named Zita is remembered as the patroness of domestic servants because of her faithfulness throughout her life. Born in 1215, she served the Fatinelli family in Italy from age twelve until her death in 1272. Bernard Mizeki, who became a lay preacher and then a martyr in 1896 in the church in Rhodesia (now Zimbabwe), began his Christian life as a house servant in South Africa.

We need to be reminded of all these people who have done their ministry in so many different ways, but we must not stop there; we need to go on in our remembering and bring into useful consciousness the stories of so many others who can be models of ministry for us today.

Ministry According to the Gifts Given Them

Our ministry is shaped by the gifts we have been given. That is quite obvious from the patterns of ministry we have seen in the lives of the people we have just considered. However, it is often harder to see our gifts in our everyday lives.

Each Christian is given gifts for ministry. One of the most important ministries a Christian congregation can give its members is to recognize and name one another's gifts and support the use of those gifts.

Most of the time the recognition of gifts is a very exhilarating experience. It is harder to recognize gifts when they involve suffering or limitations. Mary Reed, a missionary teacher from the United States, went to India in 1884 at the age of thirty. She was not physically strong but was able to teach for six years before she returned to the United States for medical treatments. There it was discovered that she had somehow contracted leprosy. She decided that this leprosy was a special gift given her by God, and she returned to India to spend the rest of her life caring for others who had leprosy. When she left her family to return to India, she did not tell them of her illness. After she arrived in India she wrote to tell them. Her letter ended, "God has enabled me to say not with a sigh, but with song, 'Thy will be done.' "[12] She became director of a leper community in Chandag, and there she preached, taught, and nursed until her death in 1943.

It is God who gives the gifts and God who intends that the gifts be used. Our responsibility as a Christian community is to be sensitive always to the gifts in our midst, especially those that seem most unlikely, and to encourage and support persons to use those gifts for God's service.

Ministry According to the Place and Time

Our ministries are also shaped by the time and place in which we live. Dag Hammerskjöld (1905-61) was secretary-general of the United Nations at a critical period in world history when many former colonies, especially in Africa, were becoming independent nations. His diary, *Markings*, published after his death, tells us the story of his sense of vocation in the place and time in which God had set him.

One of the remarkable women of modern China was Dr. Wu Yi Fang. She graduated from Ginling College in Nanjing in 1919. After completing her Ph.D. in biology at the University of Michigan, she returned to China to become president of Ginling College. She held this position until 1951 when Ginling became Nanjing Teachers' University, and she remained honorary president of that institution until a year before her death in 1985. In 1945 she was the Chinese representative, and the only woman delegate, to the founding of the United Nations. Although she was active in the

Kuomintang government, she came to support Chairman Mao because of the hope he brought for the transformation of China. She became a long-serving, elected member of the People's Congress. She was an active member of the Protestant Three Self Movement, which worked for self-support, self-government, and self-propagation among Chinese Christians. When the China Christian Council was formed in 1980, she became one of the leaders in that body. In all the twists and turns of that particular time and place, she was able to live out her unique Christian ministry.

All of these people, in using their gifts for ministry in the name of Christ, have truly been saints in the biblical sense of the word. They have used the talents and abilities given them by God in the context of life in which they found themselves. In doing so, they have carried on the life of the church as the people of God.

4

The Nature
of Ministry

Thus far, we have been reviewing various models of the ministry of the people of God—in the Bible and in Christian experience. Now it is time to determine the essential elements in this ministry to which God calls us. We find in the New Testament two models of ministry that seem to be fundamental to all the possible shapes of ministry.

One model is the *ministry of reconciliation*; the other model is the *ministry of friendship*. The classic text for the first is found in Paul's letter to the Corinthian church:

> From now on, therefore, we regard no one from a human point of view; even though we once knew Christ from a human point of view, we know him no longer in that way. So if anyone is in Christ, there is a new creation; everything old has passed away; see, everything has become new! All this is from God, who reconciled us to himself through Christ, and has given us the ministry of reconciliation; that is, in Christ God was reconciling the world to himself, not counting their trespasses against them, and entrusting the message of reconciliation to us. So we are ambassadors for Christ, since God is making his appeal through us. (2 Cor. 5:16-20)

This ministry of reconciliation is at the heart of the vocation of the baptizing community. The Episcopal *Book of Common Prayer* declares: "The mission of the Church is to restore all people to unity with God and each other in Christ." It says that the ministry of the laity in carrying out this mission is:

> to represent Christ and his Church; to bear witness to him wherever they may be; and, according to the gifts given them, to carry on Christ's work of reconciliation in the world; and to take their place in the life, worship, and governance of the Church.[1]

The *National Baptist Churchman's Handbook* affirms, "Above all things our job is the ministry of reconciliation."[2]

The second New Testament model of ministry gives us a standard for the quality of all ministry: the *ministry of friendship*. We see this most clearly in the account of what Jesus was and said and did at the Last Supper:

> This is my commandment, that you love one another as I have loved you. No one has greater love than this, to lay down one's life for one's friends. You are my friends if you do what I command you. I do not call you servants any longer, because the servant does not know what the master is doing; but I have called you friends, because I have made known to you everything that I have heard from my Father. You did not choose me but I chose you. And I appointed you to go and bear fruit, fruit that will last, so that the Father will give you whatever you ask him in my name. I am giving you these commands so that you may love one another. (John 15:12-17)

To equip the saints for ministry is to nourish and encourage the ministry of reconciliation and friendship by the people of God, person by person and as a whole community.

THE MINISTRY OF RECONCILIATION

What is reconciliation? We use this word to talk about facing up to circumstances: "I just cannot reconcile myself to this new way of thinking." Or we use it when talking about our bank accounts: "Reconciling my bank statement with my checkbook is sometimes very difficult." At other times we use it to talk about bringing persons together: "Mary and her daughter have been reconciled."

The Greek word used in the New Testament for which our word *reconciliation* is a translation is *katallasso*. This word is a combination of two words: *kata*, meaning "down from, under, in, after, against"; and *allasso*, meaning "to change, exchange (especially money)." These root meanings imply that in reconciliation something actually happens or some things change hands or position so that persons or things move to a different place in relation to each other.

This change is reflected in Paul's passage on the ministry of reconciliation in 2 Corinthians: "From now on, therefore we regard no one from a human point of view; even though we once knew Christ from a human point of view, we know him no longer in that way" (5:16). In the process of reconciliation we see the participants and the situation through quite different eyes.

The ministry of reconciliation is more than carrying out strategies or programs. "So if anyone is in Christ, there is a new creation; everything old has passed away; see, everything has become new! All this is from God, who reconciled us to himself through Christ, and has given us the ministry of reconciliation" (2 Cor. 5:17-18).

Reconciliation is the restoration and fulfillment of God's original purpose for creation. It is the people of Israel being delivered "from the Egyptians" and being brought "to a good and broad land, a land flowing with milk and honey" (Ex. 3:8). It is nations beating "swords into plowshares" and not learning war any more, but all people sitting under their own vines and fig trees, with no one to make them afraid (see Mic. 4:3-4). It is the prodigal son coming to himself and being welcomed home into a new relationship (see Luke 15:11-32).

The ministry of reconciliation is possible, not because people are institutionally commissioned to carry it out or are licensed to do this particular ministry, but because people have experienced reconciliation in their own lives and in the lives of others.

Christ's Work of Reconciliation

The Book of Common Prayer tells us that the ministry of laypersons is "to carry on Christ's work of reconciliation in the world." What does that work look like? Here are some examples from the life of Jesus:

Jesus' teaching: "You have heard that it was said to those of ancient times. . . . But I say to you. . ." (Matt. 5:21-22).

Jesus' affirmation: "The time is fulfilled, and the kingdom of God has come near" (Mark 1:15). This was said at a time when God's kingdom seemed far away.

Jesus' care for justice: "Let anyone among you who is without sin be the first to throw a stone at her" (John 8:7; see the story of the woman taken in adultery, vv. 2-11).

Jesus' company: Think of all of those who came to see and to be seen from God's point of view—for example, children, tax collectors, fishermen, women.

Jesus' death on the cross: The worst of human actions can become transformed into the vehicle of God's power and goodness and peace.

Laypersons Carry on Christ's Work of Reconciliation

Today laypersons are continuing to work for reconciliation, following Jesus. Here are some examples:

Bill is an executive in a large investment firm. When he was asked what connection he saw between what went on for him in church on Sunday and what he did for the rest of the week, he said:

> In my business there is no way or time for persons to admit that they have done wrong. But we all do. In church I learn and practice knowing that all of us make mistakes and are forgiven. That helps me to be more loving and forgiving of others and myself in the day-by-day pressures in my company.

Bill's knowledge of Christ strengthens him to be a minister of reconciliation within his firm.

Mary is a Christian laywoman who is active in local school affairs. The school board took a community survey of opinions on the high school. Because the teachers found the process and the report so threatening, a committee of parents, teachers, and students was formed to look closely at the report to explore how all could use the results creatively. Mary was asked to work with this committee. She found much confrontation within the group. Over and over she needed to help people to look at themselves and at the situation through different eyes. Mary said she could only help others do this because she had experienced other Christians looking at her "through God's eyes," and she knew God's love that way.

Corrymeela is a Christian ecumenical center of reconciliation in Northern Ireland. One of the center's projects has been the annual summer program for mentally retarded adults from Belfast who come to enjoy the healing environment of this place. The staff of Corrymeela sees this program as reconciling, as restorative of peace of mind for these persons so badly disturbed by the battling in the city. It also provides time for reconciliation in the spirits of those who care for these persons.

The Carter Center of Emory University, founded in 1982 by former United States president Jimmy Carter, uses the wisdom of policy makers and the power of successful political leaders to work toward reconciliation of intra- and international conflicts around the world. The center has worked to resolve the conflict between Ethiopia and Eritrea, and has monitored democratic elections in Zambia and Haiti. As Carter himself acknowledges, his own Christian commitment is the ground for his mission of reconciliation, so he welcomes all other peacemakers of whatever commitment into this work. He recognizes that unique gifts are needed for this work: knowledge of the needs and possibilities of people of the world, the status and power of past leadership, skills in negotiation strengthened by practice, and the ability to accept vulnerability and to be willing to fail.

Where Reconciliation Is Needed

One can all too readily think of places where reconciliation is needed in the world today. Individuals struggle with conflicting forces within themselves and too often resort to substance abuse or suicide. Some feel intense conflict between their personal ethics and the demands of their jobs.

There are many conflicts between individuals, between individuals and their community, and between groups and nations. We have come to see in recent years the need for reconciliation between our desires and the available resources of the natural world.

Ultimately, all of us need reconciliation with God, which as Paul points out, lies at the heart of all reconciliation with others and with our world.

Since the need for reconciliation is everywhere, it must largely be the ministry of the laity, the people of God. The laity find themselves at the places where there is alienation. The ministry of reconciliation can be done only by people who are at the right place at the time they are needed by those who are alienated. And those ministering must use whatever gifts they have to do the work of reconciliation.

Strengthening Laity for the Ministry of Reconciliation

There are three essential ways in which we Christians need to be prepared in order to be ambassadors of reconciliation.

Most important, we ourselves must have the experience of being reconciled. The Christian community is the place in which this can and must happen.

Over the centuries of the Christian era, Christians have tried different ways to ensure that reconciliation was practiced within the Christian community. Jesus' instructions are recorded in Matthew 5: "So when you are offering your gift at the altar, if you remember that your brother or sister has something against you, leave your gift there before the altar and go; first be reconciled to your brother or sister, and then come and offer your gift" (vv. 23-24). This practice has been continued intermittently in Christian groups that maintain public confession of personal sins. Many liturgies include a form for the common act of reconciliation, including confession and the declaration of God's forgiveness and reconciliation, which is especially important in resolving our corporate disunity. The ministry of reconciliation within the Christian community has been carried out formally and informally through those persons ordered to speak the word of God's reconciliation to those who are open to being changed. A congregation in which reconciliation is part of the pattern for worship can also become a congregation in which each Christian becomes a reconciler for others.

It is important that each member of the church continually has the experience of being in a community in which he or she feels free to say, "I have sinned and am separated from myself [or from another person or from God]." The person can then know in very concrete ways that God forgives the sin in and through this community. Only in knowing reconciliation are we able to be reconcilers.

Second, if Christians are to carry out Christ's work of reconciliation "according to the gifts given them," they need others to help them be clear and confident in the gifts they have been given and to suggest imaginative ways for them to use these gifts.

"Spiritual gifts" are those talents and abilities that have been given to each person by God to be used for God's purposes. They become spiritual gifts when we acknowledge their source and use them for their intended purpose. There is a whole range of gifts to be used in the ministry of reconciliation in our congregations: welcoming guests, planning meetings, listening, walking, baking cookies, confronting, being stubborn (or patient), doing accounting, singing, and so many more.

The church's equipping of the saints for ministry must include training in negotiation and conflict management. Too often the church is the place where we deliberately avoid conflict. So strengthening for the ministry of reconciliation can begin in our own community. We need to include training in working through conflicts with all the groups in the congregation: children, young people, church councils, and so on. The congregation may have persons such as family violence counselors and labor union leaders who have had training and experience in helping others learn how to work with conflict. All such gifts need to be used.

Third, the Christian community needs to be a place where persons are remembered and prayed for in their ministry of reconciliation. A *Peanuts* cartoon some years ago showed Snoopy taking his friends for a walk. When they came to a chasm, the only way they could get across was for him to become the bridge. The whole company walked across him and continued on its journey. Snoopy was still there when the moon came up. He reflected: "You don't think about it, but when you're a bridge you get lonely at night."

Reconcilers need to be linked. This ministry is that of the whole church, done corporately even when it is being done in the most isolated places.

The mark of a Christian community must always be that it is a gathering of the people of God in which they know they are forgiven, know they are never alone, and know they are a gifted community.

THE MINISTRY OF FRIENDSHIP

"You are my friends if you do what I command you. I do not call you servants any longer, because the servant does not know what the master is doing; but I have called you friends, because I have made known to you everything that I have heard from my Father" (John 15:14-15).

On the night before the Passover feast, Jesus and his disciples met in the upper room of a house in Jerusalem. During the meal Jesus got up from the table and carefully prepared himself to serve his disciples, taking off his outer cloak and tying a towel around his waist. He poured water into a basin and then went from disciple to disciple washing each man's feet and wiping them with the towel (see John 13:1-15).

Footwashing in that society was a very menial act of service, so unpleasant that even slaves could not be required to do it.

Peter was appalled. When Jesus came to him, he protested violently, "Lord, are you going to wash my feet?" (v. 6). Maybe the others, but not his!

Jesus said, "You do not know now what I am doing, but later you will understand" (v. 7).

But Peter proclaimed, "You will never wash my feet" (v. 8).

Jesus persisted, "Unless I wash you, you have no share with me" (v. 8).

Peter, with his usual exuberance, begged, "Lord, not my feet only but also my hands and my head!" (v. 9).

To this Jesus replied, "One who has bathed does not need to wash, except for the feet" (v. 10).

When Jesus finished washing the feet of all the men in the room, he put on his robes and sat down among them again. Then he said to them all, "Do you know what I have done to you? You call me Teacher and Lord—and you are right, for that is what I am. So if I, your Lord and Teacher, have washed your feet, you also ought to wash one another's feet. For I have set you an example, that you also should do as I have done to you" (vv. 12-15).

What was going on in that room? Do we know what Jesus was doing?

An important clue for us is the intensity of Peter's refusal to let Jesus wash his feet. Peter had refused what Jesus said before. In Caesarea Philippi when Jesus told the disciples about his necessary coming death and resurrection, Peter's response was, "God forbid, Lord. This shall never happen!" But Jesus said to Peter, "Get behind me, Satan! For you are setting your mind not on divine things but on human things" (see Mark 8:31-33). Peter's protest against Jesus washing his feet indicates that somehow he knew that what was involved here was a matter of life or death.

Jesus' response shows this too: "Unless I wash you, you have no share with me" (no inheritance in me). Here Jesus was treating Peter quite differently from the way he did after the resurrection. Then, even though Peter had denied him, Jesus still asked him to "feed my sheep" (see John 21:15-19). But the heritage could come only by letting Jesus do this incredibly simple menial act.

Jesus gave another clue in the bidding, "So if I, your Lord and Teacher, have washed your feet, you also ought to wash one another's feet" (John 13:14). By this act Jesus was giving a model of the way in which "teachers and lords" relate to others, a model for all relationships.

Jesus' Model of Relationships

Jesus' footwashing becomes a radical parable of the relationship of service, of ministry. Jesus charged his disciples—and us—to reenact this parable in spirit, if not in fact.

When one considers relationships between persons or groups, it is helpful to ask where they are placed in relationship to the others—below, above, or with. Our understanding of our place of relationship is important in helping us be clear about our ministry. Where was Jesus seen to be when he washed the feet of his disciples?

If Jesus had been a slave, probably the disciples would have seen him as beneath them. But they already called him Teacher and Lord, and he accepted those titles. Could Jesus have served them to win their love before he died? And would Peter have let him get away with that?

How often is service, or ministry, done from a position of servility? By people who are slaves, hired servants, employees? By people who are in bondage—doing ministry to ease consciences, to gain power, to win approval, to amass material goods?

Or did Jesus do this footwashing from a position above the disciples? Was the Teacher and Lord taking care of his people because there was no one else to do it for them and no one in the house had provided this service? It seems hard to believe that Peter would have been so upset by that. If that were the case, Peter might have jumped up and washed the others' feet himself.

How often is service, or ministry, done from a position above for others who are thought to be weak or ignorant or incapable of doing it for themselves? By mothers and fathers, teachers, or clergy? By first world countries and churches for two-thirds world countries and churches?

Can we say that Jesus' service was a way for him to be "with" them? It seems to have been a spontaneous act, joyously and simply carried out at the last meal Jesus was to have with his friends. It was not a necessary act. Someone else could have done it, or it could have been left undone. It was not done at a distance—Jesus got right into it, taking off his garment so he could have freedom to move.

How often is our service, or ministry, done from a position of being "along with," being "equal with"? Not from a distance, but involving our bodies and minds and spirits with those of others?

This is the ministry of friendship, the unusual service that wants nothing and needs nothing but is done just because we love the other person. Aelred, a monk who wrote a treatise on friendship in 1160, reworded the well-known saying of John (1 John 4:16) to say, "He that abides in friendship, abides in God, and God in him."[3] When Jesus washed his disciples' feet, he was bringing them in as a part of, as inheritors of, this friendship with God.

No wonder Peter was scandalized; he saw that Jesus was calling him to a whole new way of relationships. Peter was willing to bow down before Jesus and let Jesus serve him in any way the Lord chose. Actually Peter had the potential to get quite angry with Jesus when he did not do all the service Peter expected from him, such as when the disciples had to awaken Jesus when he fell asleep on the stormy sea (see Matt. 8:23-27). Now Jesus was offering a relationship of friendship, a relationship of equals that broke through such roles as Teacher and Lord. Peter did not know what to do with that, especially when Jesus said that they should do to others what he had done to them.

How do we respond to this invitation of friendship that God offers to us? How do we live out this friendship in our relationship with others?[4]

Living the Ministry of Friendship

There are as many ways to live out this ministry as there are persons and groups and organizations. Therefore, models for this ministry cannot be prescribed. However, there are certain steps we can take in strengthening ourselves to live this ministry.

First, we need continually to define ourselves to discover our particular role—for ourselves and in relation to others. It is very difficult to relate to others as equals when we feel superior or inferior to them, when we do not recognize that all are loved by God equally. This is particularly difficult when we have the responsibility of maintaining the roles of teacher, boss, CEO, parent, and pastor. Jesus' own model serves us well here.

Second, it is important to keep sight of the whole of any issue, problem, or concern no matter what "side" we are on. We must ask, "What is my/our responsibility to my/our own side?" And "What is my/our responsibility to the other side?" Asking these questions is important when considering issues such as abortion, economic inequality, apartheid, lesbian/gay rights, and drug addiction. Apply them to difficult relations in your job, home, or neighborhood.

Third, we grow in our ability to be a friend as we recognize the contradictions in the world and in ourselves. We receive help in this as we affirm Jesus as a sign of God's contradictions. Consider the way Jesus countered the expectations of his hearers. The meek will not be trampled under foot, but will inherit the earth (see Matt. 5:2-12). Or recall how he brought life when others saw death (see Mark 5:21-43). He told us not to love those who already love us, but to love our enemies (see Luke 6:32-36). The ultimate contradiction is seen in the cross, where weakness and death climaxed in resurrection and power.

This affirmation may not be easy, but living the ministry of friendship means our always being divinely discontent with small answers to large questions.

Fourth, Christians are always obligated to practice listening to others. William Diehl asks, "What's wrong with a Christian education program which offers a course in effective listening?"[5] A test of listening with understanding is being able to repeat back that which you have heard to the satisfaction of the person who spoke.

Fifth, we have to find ways to ask questions that are mutual and not threatening. We can try these out on ourselves. How would we feel if a possible new friend asked us these questions:

"Tell me about. . . ."

"How does this work. . . ?"

"What do you do when. . . ?"

"How is this different from. . . ?"

Sixth, most important is our willingness to begin with little steps. The ministry of friendship takes time. We must remember that an essential element in, and mark of, friendship is shared humor—not humor intended to destroy, but humor that comes from enjoyment of one another.

The ministry of reconciliation and the ministry of friendship are the calling of the whole people of God, privilege and responsibility. They involve both the quality of the whole of our life and specific acts that we do. Gerard Manly Hopkins said, "The just man justices."[6] So, the reconciling person reconciles and the befriending person befriends.

All particular ministries, such as teaching, healing, and advocacy, are grounded in these two "wherever, whatever, whenever, whomever" ministries.

The particular responsibility of ordained and lay leadership in strengthening laity in these ministries is to shape the church's environment in such a way that persons can:

- know that all Christians share the ministry of reconciliation and are measured by the standard of Jesus' ministry of friendship;
- experience and practice reconciliation and friendship in safe places where risking is possible;
- share their stories of living these ministries, both their faithfulness and their failures, and be given the guidance and hope to continue living them out day by day.

5

Connecting with the People

One of the saddest aspects of present attempts to fulfill the ministry of the people of God is the failure of ordained and lay leaders to share the church's resources in such a way that the laity become aware of God's call to them and are supported in responding to God. It is rather like two ships passing in a fog; the leaders have collected and studied the resources of the Bible, theology, church history, liturgy, and ethics, but they are not adept in using the material to strengthen the laity. The laity continue to accept these resources but do not know how to translate them for use in their lives day by day.

Therefore, an essential part of the task of strengthening laity in ministry is the development of Christian literacy. Christian literacy is the ability to read the stuff of our Christian faith and practice in such a way that we can connect it with what goes on in our world. The more we grow in our ability to make these connections, the more we can risk attempts at making new connections of faith and life and so grow in our effectiveness in ministry.

ISSUES IMPORTANT TO THE LAITY

Listening to the concerns of laity is a key to releasing the power of the laity for God's ministry in the whole world. Church leaders have learned a bit about relating Christian resources to church and home, mainly to primary groups. They may have some insights into such occupations as health care or social work or education. These arenas are close to the life and work of the church leaders. However, church leaders usually know very little about how to relate the resources of faith to secondary groups and the structures and systems of society.

The experience of a woman who is director of compensation research for a major bank exemplifies this failure of the church to make connections with the needs she feels on her job. She reflected:

> I like my job. I work hard at it. I think it is fun. And it's very rewarding to me. When things go well, it's wonderful. It's nice to complain sometimes, . . . but by and large, I really do get a charge out of what I do. And my church has had a difficult time, institutionally, dealing with me in these areas where I do quite well.
>
> I support and don't support programs for equal opportunities. I can treat my co-workers, my subordinates, my superiors as my equals, as real people, or I can treat them as units of production in a great financial organization. . . . My church does not seem to know much about this side of my work. I would like to see the churches relating more to the strengths and opportunities of their business members, to their areas where they excel, rather than waiting as it were until they lose their jobs, and then moving in to comfort and counsel with them.
>
> My whole feeling is that I like my job. I feel it is a responsible one, and I want to work out my Christian responsibilities in it. I do not find that my local church, or the churches in my city, really know how to help me do this.[1]

Christians spend the bulk of their time and energy in situations like this in which the issues seem remote from what they hear in church. In recent years, an increasing number of people have left such positions to seek ordination as clergy in their churches. Ironically, their influx into the ordained leadership of the church has not increased significantly the church's ability to strengthen laity in their secular occupations. Too often the "second career" clergy and lay professionals choose to change careers because they have been unable to find a sense of meaningful ministry in their secular jobs. If they have not been able to find a fulfilling ministry as a lawyer, engineer, manager, or salesperson, they are not inclined to expect it from those in their parish.

Students in a course entitled Strengthening Laity in Ministry given at the Graduate Theological Union in Berkeley, California, were asked to interview lay people. The questions to be used were adapted from the work of Dr. Nelvin Vos:[2]

- What is your daily activity? How many people do you meet in that daily activity?
- What are the instances of decision making, pressure, and tension in your main daily activity?
- What are the instances of feeling right with the world and celebrating in your main daily activity?
- What, if any, connection is there between what goes on in your church and in your main daily activity?

The students found that the interviewees were delighted to talk about their occupations. They said things like "I didn't think the church was interested in what I do at work." Some interviewees at first had difficulty in grasping that what they do on the job can be ministry. Most who were visited at the workplace said they had never received a visit from clergy at their jobs.

What are some of the issues these California laity said they face in their daily lives?

- uncertainty over the future;
- competitiveness among colleagues;
- aggressive, unreconciling Christianity and how to respond to it;
- obstacles to change in the system;
- truth-falsehood dilemmas in ethical decisions, especially when systems push "unethical" decisions;
- hierarchies, in medical systems especially, but in other systems as well;
- heavy pressures and expectations;
- being torn in two trying to keep job frustrations at the workplace and yet needing people and places to share them;
- being overwhelmed by the needs for ministry, for meeting crises;
- time management as an overwhelming problem;
- pride in work versus humility;
- personal goals and God's goals.

To engage in the task of developing Christian literacy requires a great deal of listening to laypersons tell of the issues that are tearing into them in the whole of their lives.

Lay people often find great satisfaction in their daily lives. When the seminary students asked the interviewees in California, "What are the instances of feeling right with the world and celebrating in your main daily activity?" these were some of the answers:

- working with kids, making a breakthrough into a family,

- coming up with new ideas,
- doing a good job,
- forming relationships with people,
- seeing things "all come together" and seeing all people help with that—"serendipitous,"
- getting positive feedback, receiving kind comments, and having someone to care,
- being significant.

Probably few of these lay people had translated these experiences as expressions of the "abundant life" Jesus came to give.

RELATING THEOLOGICAL INSIGHTS TO DAILY OCCUPATIONS

As we continue to listen with all our senses to the realities that laity experience in their specific occupations—and in their leisure, home life, and political and economic activities as well—we must recognize that they are talking about profound needs. This is where theology, the talk of God begins. This linkage of theological insights to the pressures, tensions, and also the triumphs in daily activity is a critical step in developing Christian literacy.

How are theological insights linked to the realities of daily experience? Let us take for an example the study Jan Halper of the Palo Alto Consulting Center did of more than four thousand male business executives.[3]

- Forty-eight percent of all middle managers said that despite years spent striving to achieve their professional goals, their lives seemed "empty and meaningless."
- Sixty-eight percent of senior executives said that they had neglected their family lives to pursue professional goals, and half said they would spend less time working and more time with their wives and children if they could start over again.
- Five out of seven managers said they preferred not to offer their employees constructive criticism. Among the reasons: They were afraid of not being liked, they did not know how to provide helpful criticism, and they simply hoped that the employees would improve over time.

Some of these executives and others like them are probably members of our congregations. How do we understand what they are expressing? When working and teaching in a culture with a language different from our own, we must listen with all our senses, not just our ears, to what others are expressing. Then we have to play with their expressions in our own language to see where the links are between our world and theirs. Only then can we have the communion necessary for sharing. Those who talk the language of Christian resources have to listen with all their senses to the response of laity in order to transmit to them the power of this material.

Too often, those who have been theologically educated have been afraid to share theological insights with laity, thinking that those concepts were irrelevant to their lives—and often when they were shared, the manner in which they were presented did make them irrelevant. However, in this time of enormous and fearful change when world events seem so beyond our understanding and control, people grab at whatever answers to the questions of life are available and easily assimilated, such as "shoulder patch" patriotism, video war games, impending last judgments, and fundamentalisms of the left or right.

Many, many Christians are looking for more than this. They want to know what the difference is between the church and the Rotary Club, between being a Christian and being a good person. As a number of laity said in seminars for persons working in the business and corporate worlds, "Do not tell us what to do as Christians, but help us know what are the bases for our actions as Christians and help us to form groups with other Christians so we are not alone in our actions." What are the basic affirmations of the Christian faith that will serve them as grounding for the meaning and motive of life?

First, the Christian faith provides a confidence about the ultimate meaning of existence. Justification by grace through faith is sometimes called the "gift of meaning." All our striving for achievement may be fine as long as we recognize that ultimate meaning can be provided only by faith. Certainly, there is the ground for hope because of God's demonstrated power to bring freedom out of slavery and life out of death. What difference does our celebration of Easter make unless we can relate it to the way we confront the seemingly uncontrollable in our domestic life, our cities, our economy, and our international relations?

Second, the Book of Genesis affirms that God created human beings in God's image. To be made in God's image is to be made a picture of God for all of creation. All human beings have to resolve the question, whether or not they realize it in just these terms, of what kind of picture of God they are going to be. The Bible records that in order to help all human beings be the image of God, one people, the Hebrew people, were chosen as a pilot study. God worked especially with them to show God's self and God's purposes so they could faithfully represent (or re-present) God to the whole world. Christians understand that their baptism includes them in this pilot study with the same end, that they may grow in the way they represent God to the world with ever greater accuracy and strength. What does it mean to represent God in a primary school as a student or teacher, in the hospital as a doctor or nurse or patient, or in an unemployment office as an employee or applicant? How do we encounter the other as one also made in the image of God? When the majority of the world's population is starving and sick and homeless, what kind of picture of God are we seeing?

Another facet of knowing that we have been created in the image of God is the awareness that we are part of the community that God is creating. We can begin to sort out the relationships between the various human communities of which we are a part. The satisfaction that comes from belonging to a community of faith, a family, or a group of friends need not be at odds with loyalty to the firm that employs us. Open discussion of the mutual respect for each relationship can be mutually affirming.

Third, the Christian faith roots the meaning or justification of each person's existence in the affirming love of God. Even if we do not have this assurance of personal worth or cannot bring it to the workplace, we still need it. So when any of us—executives, managers, parents, politicians, or students—seek to find this affirming love from co-workers, colleagues, or children, we may be looking in the wrong place. If we know that the justification of our life is a gift from God, we will not fear that we will risk losing it by giving constructive criticism or being honest in all of our relationships.

Robert Bellah, in a lecture on "Discipleship and Citizenship in the Workplace," says: "Professional today too often means merely expertise, narrowly defined competence; and the professional in that sense can often be arrogant and insensitive to those presumably not on the same elite level. But the older and deeper meaning of profession was closely associated with the idea of vocation, or calling."[4] Christians are told to "lead a life worthy of the calling to which you have been called" (Eph. 4:1). How might Christians walk in their jobs, leisure, community, and national affairs so that all persons they meet will know they can make a difference in the world? Retired Bishop of Winchester John Taylor has said on many occasions, "Mission is finding out what God is doing in the world and doing it with God." Over the centuries the biblical idea of calling was restricted to those persons who decided to be ordained and become professional Christian leaders. Now all Christians have the responsibility to take back the full biblical sense of the "calling" that belongs to all the people of God. Some will recognize that relationship, and others may be like Cyrus, king of Persia, who fulfilled God's purposes even when he did not recognize the God of Israel.

Fourth, a healthy understanding of sin and the renewing power of forgiveness is essential grounding for living the Christian faith today. We need to be honest with the sinfulness that gets mixed with all our attempts at faithfulness in our own lives. We also need to accept that there is sinfulness in the lives of all those around us. Just "being nice" is not enough. The acceptance of the fact of sin in our world may well be welcome relief, for it strengthens us to be able to admit to mistakes and stop covering up our transgressions. Also, while it helps us sort out mountains and molehills, it also aids us in coping with confusion and despair when all goes wrong. But we cannot stop there. Christians believe that forgiveness is always available when we truly repent. So not only are we given renewal through confession and the assurance of forgiveness, but we are also then able to be channels of this forgiveness to those around us.

THEOLOGICAL EDUCATION OF THE LAITY

Most parts of the Christian church have taken seriously the need to provide quality theological education for those to be ordained as its leaders. However, there has been little concern to provide theological education for laity. What education we have provided we have called "Christian education" or "religious education," and we have rarely been serious about this endeavor. In most times such education is directed primarily toward children and youth.

Therefore, if we are to cultivate literate Christians, we have to institute a radically different approach to theological education. We begin with the assumption that the center of theological education is in the local congregation. All programs of theological education either for those who will be ordained or for those laypersons who will be employed in the work of the church community, whether they take place in residential seminaries and colleges or in extension programs, are to equip persons to teach, lead, and staff the centers of theological education in local congregations. Such centers will engage in theological education of all the people—from the very youngest to the oldest. They will use many different formats and times and places for theological education. There may be such long-term educational programs as Kerygma or Bethel Bible Series or the four-year Sewanee Education for Ministry course.[5] However, such programs can provide theological education only to a select number of persons who have the resources to undertake such study. Theological education that will develop literate Christians has to take place in youth programs and parents' groups, in classes for the preparation of receiving the newly baptized, in sermons and church council meetings that focus on the congregation's outreach projects.

What goes into this theological education of the laity? There are eight ways in which Christians need to be growing in lifelong in-service training in ministry. By framing these eight ways as questions, we can use them as guides and standards by which we plan and evaluate the work of the congregation as a center of theological education.

1. How can we read the biblical story of God's covenant with the people of God so that we can know God's covenant with us today?

2. What does it mean to be a Christian? Who is Jesus Christ? How have people answered that question in the past? How do we answer that question today? What are some alternative ways of making meaning in our world? How do we choose the way for us?

3. How does God view creation? How do we view it?

4. What are the issues about which we have to make decisions in our public and private lives today? What is involved in these issues? How do we apply our Christian beliefs and perspectives to these issues?

5. How have others lived out their Christian commitments throughout the history of the church?

6. How do we recognize God at work in our world today so we can join in God's work?

7. What is involved in participation in the Christian community? What is the church? How do I/we participate? Who am I? Who are you? How do we make community? How do we worship? Especially as the royal priesthood, how do we offer the world to God?

8. How do we grow in our communion with God? What can help us in this growth?

Also, provision for training in a variety of ministry skills will be needed. Again, these must be fashioned for persons of different ages engaged in ministry in different places. For example, we have already noted that the ministry of reconciliation is a basic ministry of all Christians.

What skills are needed for this ministry? Certainly, listening and conflict management/resolution are necessary. So is the practice of being the royal priesthood, of offering the conflicted world and persons to God.

Christians are called to tell the good news of Jesus Christ in a variety of situations. Can we equip primary school children to do this? parents? businesspersons? How can we equip laity to be givers of pastoral care? We can train young people or older people to be peer counselors with those of their own generation.

CLERGY/OCCUPATION DIALOGUES

Dialogues between clergy and persons in a given profession or occupation have real value in helping persons make the connection between the resources of the Christian faith and their own life concerns. Occupations can be defined to include those who are paid workers, those whose primary daily activity is in the home, and those who are retired, volunteers, or unemployed. The March 1989 issue of *Initiatives* reported on "The Dialogue Between the Religious and Labor Community on Social and Ethical Concerns in a Changing Economy," which was held in January 1989 in Washington, D.C. Monsignor George Higgins called it "the most important meeting of its kind in my lifetime." This same issue of *Initiative* also reported on a group of more than three hundred business leaders who met with church leaders in St. Louis "not to discuss what they could do for the Church but to discuss how Church leaders might meet the religious needs of women and men in industry and business."[6]

In March 1989 the Center for Ethics and Social Policy of the Graduate Theological Union in Berkeley, California, asked Otto Bremer to set up a "Clergy/Business Dialogue." He decided on an experiential approach: he asked corporations to sponsor one or two executives who would attend a day-long seminar and bring their clergyperson with them. Some of the CEOs did not quite understand why such a dialogue was important, but others did. The twenty-five persons who spent that Thursday together were enthusiastic. The day provided opportunity for identifying issues, hearing presentations by an economist and a theologian, and discussing a case study. The clergy later spent a day at the workplace of the executive. Then the group came together again in two months to compare experiences.

It turned out that in spite of agreement by the participants to the visits to executive offices by the clergy, this part of the project was not very successful. The idea of a clergyperson "shadowing" the executive for a day on the job was difficult to realize. As the clergy/executive teams reported, it was clear that greater understanding of the work of the executives was gained but only one clergyperson really "shadowed" the businessperson. The clergy did get a better view of the work of the executives and were more appreciative of the influence their decisions had. Teams of clergy and businesspersons need to try a variety of ways to improve understanding of each other's workplace ministry.

Another way to develop understanding of the daily work and environment of laity was undertaken by an Episcopal priest who spent a sabbatical working for two three-month periods in two of his parishioners' workplaces. The lay persons were greatly surprised by their rector's asking to do this. It took time and imagination to work it out, but the experience was very valuable to all involved.

Seminary students whose assignment is to interview lay persons say repeatedly how valuable it is to interview the laity in their workplace, for they gain an understanding of the gifts and the tasks of these laity that they don't receive when they interview in the home or in the church setting.

Dialogue between clergy and other occupational groups can be held as the American Baptist Churches did with teachers and professional church leaders in the summer of 1989.

The Zadok Institute in Melbourne, Australia, "is a national study and research center concerned with examining contemporary issues in Australia in the light of biblical and theological truth. . . . Set up in 1976 in Canberra, the seat of national government in Australia, Zadok aims to equip Australians to live their faith more effectively in everyday life in Australia."[7] Several years ago the Institute brought together a group of leading economists to critique Christian material on economics in the light of their own knowledge and experience. The theologians' task was to provide resources from the Christian tradition and support the economists as they moved beyond critique to connecting those resources with the challenges of the economic domain.

Such work can be a model for authentic mutual ministry. It can be pursued with those engaged in housework, those trying to make sense of being unemployed, or young people in school.

WORKPLACE SEMINARS

When a number of churches cosponsor a seminar on the ministry of the laity, it may be possible to bring together those attending in general occupational groupings such as health care, education, business, and law. Professional church leaders, lay and ordained, can be divided among the groups.

Each group can spend a half hour brainstorming the things they do on the job that they would classify as ministry and with which their priest or pastor could help them. This process usually goes very well. Lay people will report on opportunities to share their faith with co-workers, on occasions when they respond to personal or family crises, and times when they listen to other people's problems. Some will say that they have had opportunities in their occupation or through the congregation to become better at their ministries.

Then the task is changed. Next each group is to take a half hour to identify the things they do on the job that they would call ministry but are the kind of things with which they would not expect their pastor or lay professional to be very knowledgeable about. Usually this section starts slowly and further explanations are requested. How could it be "ministry" if the "minister" cannot help me? A few examples are often needed:

- The manager who is trying to do performance appraisals in a way that will be both honest and affirming of the employee.
- The head nurse who wants the scheduling of nursing shifts to be fair and yet accommodating to personal needs.
- The teacher who must deal with poorly prepared racial minorities in a way that includes justice for all.

The results can be exciting for the laity who begin to see concrete ministry within the daily activities of their occupations. It also opens the eyes of the lay and ordained professionals who, seeing ministry through different lenses, can begin to imagine links by which they can share the resources that will strengthen laity in ministry.

6

Strengthening the Spirit for Ministry

In this book I have suggested many resources for releasing the gifts of all Christians for God's mission. These are directed toward equipping minds, bodies, and spirits. It is surprising that the strengthening of spirits seems the most difficult, because that is what the institutional church is supposed to know most about. But that is precisely why it is so difficult: Our whole culture assumes that the life of the spirit is what the church is about and that the rest of life is concerned with the real, material world.

There is gnawing evidence of people's longing for abundant life and also much confusion about what that might be and how to attain, or even obtain, it. Religious communities throughout the world, Christian and Hindu, Jewish and Islamic, ethnic and Buddhist, have restored old ways and created new resources of spirituality. They have suggested different modes of spirituality and often have combined individual and group patterns for using these resources. People have also searched for abundant life in many nonreligious ways: art, music, movies, athletic events, daring feats, violence, and even the arousal of a community through warfare.

Unfortunately, too often the separation of worlds remains. I was reminded of this acutely each year in the course I taught in Berkeley when the students reported that most laypersons saw little or no connection between what they did in church and their daily activities. If they did see a connection, it was mostly that in church they were given strength to go back and survive in the difficult world. Many of these seminarians themselves had opted for a full-time vocation in the church because they wanted a place where "they could serve God full time."

The worship of the Christian community is a critical place for the ordained and lay leaders to work with all the people of God toward uniting the worlds of head and heart, the secular and the sacred, the natural and the supernatural. This cannot be done by religious professionals alone. However, there are ways in which the religious professionals can give leadership to this process. This chapter will suggest some of these ways.

WORSHIP

The royal priesthood is reconstituted week by week as it comes to worship God. Probably nothing is more important for the strengthening of this priesthood than the form and conduct of that worship.

Worship is the act of walking between earth and heaven, the middle ground of the royal priesthood. Our offering to God of ourselves and of all of the created world that our lives have touched is changed, re-created, for us to use as God's gift to the whole of God's world. Worship is created by the Holy Spirit. Many different instruments are used in this act— music, paintings, architecture, sculpture, words, silence, books, water, bread and wine, and body movements. All are vehicles for the movement of worship.

The worship leaders are to make available all the possible resources for this exchange and to lead the members of the royal priesthood in this holy dance. The royal priesthood does the worship.

What components need to be present in worship to make it a living reality in people's lives? First, it must be linked to daily life in the world. We celebrate our joys and offer up our difficulties to God in specific terms. One congregation had in the church entrance pictures of all its members taken in the places where they spent most of their time—school room, office, field, police car, hospital room, home, legislative assembly. The display was a vivid reminder to the royal priesthood of all the world they brought with them when they came to worship. Leaders of inter-cessory prayers can make vivid the world we offer to God by including prayers that spell out specifics about all the sorts and conditions of human beings. It is important to examine the implications of the prayers to be used. For example, in the *Book of Common Prayer* there is a prayer for church musicians and artists, but when do we offer to God for God's continuing re-creation the work of *all* musicians and artists, playwrights, and television broadcasters?

Worship also needs to allow for the offering of thanksgivings for all that God has done for us day by day. Often worshipers are asked to name specific persons or events for whom or which they are thankful and those for whom or which they want to pray. It is easier to pray for those in trouble or need or for families of those who have died. How rarely we hear prayers for an upcoming company board meeting or thanksgivings for a court decision than can improve the quality of the schools in our state.

Central to the worship of the covenant people of Israel was the offering of the firstfruits of their labors to the Lord. Such offerings are still made in agricultural communities where money is scarce. Thus, there remains for these people a concrete reminder that at the heart of our worship is the offering of all of our lives. We need to find ways to make possible the offerings of the daily lives of those in urban communities. Some congregations have designed rituals in which doctors offer stethoscopes and teachers their books, computer programmers bring disks, and managers bring their weekly calendars. More work needs to be done in exploring ways in which such connections can be enhanced.

Attention also must be given to the ways in which the royal priesthood bears the re-created world as it moves from church space and time into the many spaces of daily life. Communal worship is at a particular time and place, but we need to pay attention to how that changes all times and places.

Signs and symbols and their combination in ritual are very powerful for envisioning. Signs are shorthand ways of giving us specific information, such as a road sign that tells us which way to go or a cross on a building that tells us it is a church. Symbols can have many meanings. For example, a cross is a symbol as well as a sign. As we use the cross and respond when we encounter it, we dig ever deeper into its meanings and their power for our life. The act of sharing food is a ritual, made up of many symbols, which can take on more meaning as we participate in it. Envisioning happens as we participate and gain greater knowledge through signs and their meanings. We may even create new rituals and signs.

The word *ministry* can be both a sign and a symbol. Some years ago when a friend of mine was about to retire, she arranged with her pastor that in the Sunday service she would make a public commitment to this new ministry of retirement using her church's worship form for *Commitment to Christian Service*. One congregation had a service of thanksgiving for the twenty-one-year ministry of parents whose children had attained their twenty-first birthday. We need times to offer to God particular ministries: the ministry of young people as careful drivers when they receive their first license, the ministry of teachers and students and parents as a new school year begins, the ministry of businesspersons as the Christmas season begins.

Lay people need to identify and make available the materials; the stories; the questions; the experiences; the symbols, signs, and actions; and the traditions of their world. Professional leaders need to make available the resources of the tradition. Together they weave these strands into the whole cloth of liturgy.

Not all Christians are comfortable with their corporate calling to offer the whole of God's world in worship or with the assumption that worship is the responsibility of all God's people. From the beginning of Christian teaching there has been temptation to separate world and church, secular and sacred, and to name the former bad and the latter good. However, that was certainly not the teaching of the Hebrew covenant nor of God's incarnation in Jesus Christ. Likewise, from the very beginning the church has been understood as a corporate entity of which Jesus Christ is the Head and members are the parts. The designation as royal priesthood gives the Christian congregation a particular definition of its responsibility. Most people have been taught this once, but it is critical that this teaching be done and redone with those traveling along the Christian way. Especially is this so in relation to worship, for what we learn about worship as children is quite different from the worship of young people and of adults.

This does not mean that we need to be constantly trying out new forms of worship. Power comes by steady deepening of understanding of what we are doing rather than by constant surprises. This deepening requires teaching. Both professional leaders and lay people need to teach in worship and at other times so that communal worship and daily activities interact with and interpret each other.

The quality of worship leadership is critical to the royal priesthood's offering of the whole world to God. When leaders allow themselves to become the focal point of worship, they get in the way of worship. When there is little planning or sense of direction in worship, when it is conducted sloppily or casually, there is almost no support of the royal priesthood by the worship. What is needed are not new gimmicks or dramatic changes in the order of service. Rather, the essential element of worship leadership is for leaders to recognize their role as servants in the exchange between God and the royal priesthood and be trustworthy in fulfilling this role.

Decisions must also be made about the time and place of worship. Since the beginnings of the church, Christians have used the morning of the first day of the week to celebrate corporately the resurrection of Jesus Christ. However, when Christians have lived in societies where another day was appointed for holy celebrations, such as in Islamic societies, the corporate worship has been done on that day. And worship often is conducted at different times to meet societal needs. Each Christian community needs to be conscious of the times when the whole people of God in that place can be most represented. Sunday morning may be best for middle-class suburban families, but what about those churches whose members are mainly single parents with jobs and family responsibilities for whom Sunday morning is the only time for the family to be together? A church near the university campus in Berkeley, California, has its main university community service at ten o'clock on Sunday evening. A church in Hong Kong whose people are mostly taxi drivers and hotel workers meets on Sunday evenings when most members can be present.

We must also consider the places for worship. What kind of physical environment supports the royal priesthood in worship? Are there times when we need to consider worshiping in places other than churches so that the whole people of God may take part? How can we fashion the place of worship in a nursing home so that all the people there can participate in worship? It would be helpful for us to make a long list of all the different places people have worshiped throughout the history of the people of God. We could then compare this with the places in our community today that might be alternative places for the people of God to worship. These sites are not needed in place of our churches but in addition to them, as active reminders that the full worship of the church happens only when all the people of God can take part in it.

WELCOMING THE SABBATH—SANCTIFYING TIME

Probably the most enslaving burden we bear today is the pressure of time or rather of all the demands and responsibilities crushing relentlessly into finite amounts of time. We think of this as a modern phenomenon, but time has always been a critical fact of human life. This is certainly as true in agricultural societies as in urban ones, although each feels the effects of time differently.

In the agricultural civilization of ancient Babylon, the seventh, fourteenth, twenty-first, and twenty-eighth days of every month were set aside as "days of quieting the heart."[1] Semitic culture considered seven as an evil number, so refraining from labor on those days, multiples of seven, was to safeguard against mishap from evil forces. The Hebrew people found this negative response to time also among the Canaanite people, and after receiving the Ten Commandments, they observed the Sabbath, the seventh day, as a special day.

However, because Israel was rooted in covenant with God who made the whole world, including every moment of time, they saw the seventh day as a day of joy, the day of the Lord. They knew it was God's gift for God's people. Their great poem of creation in Genesis 1-2 celebrates God's resting on the seventh day of creation.

"Resting on the seventh day" was integral to the covenant; at times the Jews made the seventh day the primary institution for keeping the covenant. However, it was always more than that, for Israel's responsibility for keeping the Sabbath as God's chosen people was in order that all of creation would experience time as God's gift. Observance of the seventh day was not a means of fighting off evil forces.

Not only did Israel celebrate the day of the Lord every week; Leviticus 25 tells us that they also set aside every seventh year as the "sabbath of the land." Some persons in our urban society keep "sabbatical" times, but then it was for land and animals as well as people. The ultimate Sabbath celebration was the Year of Jubilee, every fiftieth year, set by seven times seven plus one, which is also described in Leviticus 25. This was a time when liberty was proclaimed throughout the land to all its inhabitants: liberty from hard and relentless labor, from debts, from being separated from the land on which they were born. Every fifty years meant that ideally in the lifetime of every person there would be one Year of Jubilee. The sabbath year and the Year of Jubilee were to be constant reminders that all of creation belonged to God and not to human beings. Although scholars question if these were ever observed, the idea became part of the vision of the coming of the Messiah.

So when Jesus went to the synagogue in Nazareth and interpreted the words of Isaiah as his own vocation, he proclaimed that "the acceptable year of the Lord," the fulfillment of all time was happening at last (Luke 4:16-21). He brought this to actuality throughout his earthly ministry in the specific ways in which he kept the Sabbath. He always treated the Sabbath as God's gift for God's people, never people as God's gift for the Sabbath. Sabbaths were times for freeing people from pain and hunger. Sabbath times, "stopping times," were taken early in the morning away from the crowds, in the boat during a storm, by visiting friends, in giving self into God's hands on the cross.

Jesus received God's gift of Sabbath, and his ministry was to share that gift with the whole world. In the new covenant we share that gift and take part in that ministry.

How do we receive God's gift of the Sabbath? A first step for Christians is to acknowledge that the celebration of Sabbath and the celebration of Jesus' resurrection are two distinct observances, both important. That was quite clear in the early church when many Christians were also Jews who continued to keep the Sabbath on the seventh day and the Easter feast on Sundays.

Thus Christians need to understand the fullness of the Sabbath tradition. It is too easy to have distorted and limited ideas from fragmentary Bible reading. Especially do we need to explore the way in which the Sabbath is God's way of making all time holy by being a reminder that all time is God's time. Living in covenant with God, we have been freed from the chains of time as a vehicle by which evil forces control us, as the Babylonians and Canaanites believed.

The Israelites heard the good news of Sabbath in an agricultural context. They were to celebrate it—whether as a day or year or the Year of Jubilee. Observing the Sabbath meant stopping what they were doing and arranging in their care of family, herds, and trade. How can we receive the gift of Sabbath in the twentieth century? We have to make Sabbath by stopping in the middle of our busy lives.

Sabbath is the time for remembering that this is God's world. Making Sabbath is taking time for that remembering. One friend with a busy family life set aside one chair in his living room which he called a "Sabbath chair." His family knew that when he sat there he was not to be disturbed, for this was time he was making for God. He encouraged other family members to have their own Sabbath places and the whole family to set aside some time each week at the family table to welcome the Sabbath into their home. Making Sabbath is taking time for gardening in God's earth, for remembering God's "tinkering" with atoms as we tinker with a car, for celebrating artistic and musical gifts in a museum or concert, for playing with children, for sitting with a friend who is dying, for resting for a few minutes at our desk at midday letting God's power pour over us, or for just standing still at times. Sabbath can be a moment or a whole year or a once-in-a-lifetime stopping.

A very busy woman executive said, "Prayer is being present to God. You get it where you can." For her, strengthening comes from being present to Christ in the people she meets.

Although practicing time management may be a very important part of making Sabbath, ultimately what matters is trusting that God is in control of the world. Charles Péguy, a French poet who was killed in World War I, wrote in his poem "Sleep" that God speaks to those "who work well and sleep badly":

> They can't be resigned to trust my wisdom for the space of one night
> With the conduct and the governing of their business.
> As if I wasn't capable, if you please, of looking after it a little,
> Of watching over it,
> I have a great deal more business to look after, poor people, I govern
>   creation, maybe that is more difficult.
> . . . .
> I am talking of those who work
> And in this obey my commandment,
> And don't sleep, and who in this
> Refuse all that is good in my creation,
> Sleep, all the good I have created,
> And also refuse my commandment just the same.[2]

Also Christians share in Christ's ministry of proclaiming the "acceptable year of the Lord." What difference would it make if our business and community and family life were structured so that every person would have a sabbatical time? It would dictate that labor is good and God intends that every person have the opportunity to work creatively for the sake of the whole world. How do we make possible a sabbatical of the land? Just to begin asking how we might keep the Sabbath in our daily activities is the beginning of proclaiming that all time is God's and is to be used for God's purposes.

How does the Christian community celebrate Sabbath? One congregation planned a "stopping" time of three hours at the church every Saturday morning. No other activities were planned in the church or hall or garden for that time. People could come and go and talk with others if this was mutually agreed upon. Some have suggested that congregations might take a sabbatical year during which all program activities stop and the congregation puts itself in the hands of the Lord. As we learn how to keep the Sabbath in our personal lives and in our Christian community, we will be able to give a hallowed time to the world of our daily activity.

Since Christians do not have much experience in this practice of the Sabbath, we need to be open to the way in which God is leading us in using this gift. Time is not something mysterious or separate from our "real world"; it is with us and around us, and minute by minute we are given the possibility of making Sabbath and of sharing the gift of Sabbath with others.

GOD'S PRESENCE IN ALL THE REALMS OF LIFE

The Christian church bears a terrible responsibility for hindering the possibilities for abundant life that Jesus Christ came to give to all persons. We have yielded to the temptation to say that only certain places and objects, particular persons and actions, are sacred, thereby stating that others are outside God's realm. The Christian community has done this at the same time it asks each Christian to affirm: "I believe in God, the Father almighty, creator of heaven and earth." Therefore, the people of God need to begin taking seriously the fact that God is present "all over the map" of our lives.

This conviction, which is part of our inheritance from our Hebrew forebears, is filled up as God takes on the body of this world in Jesus Christ. Therefore, whatever we touch and handle and are involved in during our daily lives, are the areas in which God can meet us.

While we Christians can affirm this with our reason, often we do not live out this knowledge in our lives. All of us need to live in the expectation that our daily life is "the matter for contemplation," that there God meets us. Such expectation is a change from our traditional way of understanding the world. The traditional way is something like the assumptions of much of the nineteenth-century missionary movement: the church in Europe and America sent missionaries to take the God of Jesus Christ to "the heathen" who had never known God. What we have come to understand, often from the experience of the missionaries themselves, is that the God of Jesus Christ is already there and we are to be open to meeting God through those people.

This expectation of meeting God in all God's world requires expansion of the church's traditional practice of private devotion, much of which has grown up out of the long tradition of monastic prayer. Most formal theological education today still encourages training and practice in that tradition. It is good that this is so, especially for those persons who will eventually be in leadership positions in the Christian community and need to take time to develop all the resources they can to share with the people of God.

However, not many laypersons can practice the daily round of prayer and Bible reading, and even if all could, the Christian community also needs the resources that come from contemplation on the matter of daily life.

A Vietnamese poet, Thich Nhat Hanh, has written:

Wash the dishes relaxingly, as though each bowl is an object of contemplation. Consider each bowl as sacred. Follow your breath to prevent your mind from straying. Do not hurry to get the job over with. Consider washing the dishes as the most important thing in life.

Washing the dishes is meditation. If you cannot wash the dishes in mindfulness, neither can you meditate while sitting in silence.[3]

The places and persons and actions of daily life in which we can meet and be met by God are beyond number. They are the people we meet, the decisions and tensions we experience, the books and flowers and steel and bandages and money we handle, the sounds of birds and music and motors that surround us, the creativity of artists and writers and technologists that enriches our lives. What limits us in our meeting God in all of God's world is our misunderstanding that God is found only in special places.

At the same time it is essential that we do know that there are particular places where we do meet God. We need to know what that experience is like so we will recognize God in all the other places where God is. The church's leaders have a particular responsibility to make sure there are places where each person in the congregation can have the experience of meeting God. Through meeting God in the special times and places of worship, they can begin to recognize God in all the times and places of life.

PERSONAL AND SPIRITUAL RESOURCES

In a lay training program some years ago the lay students met with the clergy from their home congregation. The format of the meeting was organized around three questions directed to each of the laity and the clergy:

1. What do the laity (clergy) do that you hope they will keep on doing?

2. What do the laity (clergy) do that you wish they would do more of?

3. What do the laity (clergy) do that you wish they would do less of?

In talking with the laity before the meeting, one student said, with a certain bitterness, "I bet that what the clergy will say we should do more of is give money."

When the actual exchange took place, there was real revelation. No one mentioned money. Probably the most significant answer was the response of one of the clergy to the question, "What do the laity do that you wish they would do more of?" He said, "I wish the laity would tell more of the stories of their faith journeys so I could tell them the story of my faith journey."

In a study Jean Haldane made of religious pilgrimages of both lay and clergy, an important finding was the response from all that they had never before been asked about their religious pilgrimage or journey. "Who would ask?" said one. "Who would listen?" Her report indicates that Christians believe that while church leaders can be resources in times of great personal crises, "each person . . . is taking his or her own route, working out his salvation with varying degrees of 'fear and trembling.' Their personal religious journeys *are* personal, not shared with many, not even those close."[4]

In the course Strengthening Laity in Ministry at the Graduate Theological Union, we invited laypersons to share with the class their assessment of spiritual resources they had found helpful for their ministry and those they wished were available to them.

Several persons indicated that they had taken part in groups in which personal religious journeys were shared, such as Cursillo, Marriage Encounter, Bible study fellowships—places and times for listening to others tell stories of what happened in their lives.

Others were given strength by pastors. They listed "preaching sermons that pose questions and stimulate me to search for my own questions," "taking a personal interest in me and helping me develop my potential," and "telling us what works in being Christian in our lives." For others, strength came through participating in such activities as providing sanctuary for refugees and demonstrating for justice and peace. Listening to and making music, participating in family liturgies, and exercising were all cited as times of spiritual resourcing in busy lives. For some, time spent in religious communities such as Taizé in France or those closer to home was very important.

A young woman doctor whose husband was also a doctor said that the retreats, day-long or several days, arranged by her congregation were essential life-giving times for them. She said that an integral component of this renewal was that other members of the congregation provided child care during these retreats so that all who wanted to do so could participate.

All these lay people said that people are the greatest resource: "both people I want to be like and those I do not want to be like." For a number, early family influences have been a resource for their ministry.

What are the spiritual resources laity wish they could draw on for their ministry? Laity expressed the need for resources that can help with every-day living—struggling to meet bills that are due, working with difficult co-workers, making the best of disappointing marriage and family situations, and coping with loneliness. Here it is critical that there be fostering of groups of Christians in which there can be openness, time for confession and forgiveness, and celebration of God's grace in day-by-day journeys.

One woman said that she wanted personal help: "I didn't know how to ask for it when my husband died. I'd been the caretaker, and I didn't know how to receive." A group of women employed outside the home said they needed help with stress and burn-out. "It doesn't have to be a long time," they said, "but something to enrich us." Others requested videos and other demonstrations on everyday Christian living. For many, books of all kinds have been important, and they find it good to be able to learn of books from others. Further, a number of these persons want books that are brief and pertain to daily Christian living.

Patrick M. Arnold has expressed the concern of many that in present religious life, "the spirit of the ordinary, the familiar and the comfortably average has begun to replace imagination, initiative and risk." He describes the "masculine voice of spirituality that we need so much to hear" as "the call to leave productive enough commitments for new challenges, comfortable relationships for risky meetings with strangers, and proven ways for new viewpoints." It is Jesus' call "to leave family, home, possessions for the sake of the Kingdom of God . . . the call not to peace, but to the sword." Both are essential: God's feminine sensitivity to the personal and interrelationship, to sharing and caring, and God's masculine comforting, challenging, power-filled voice.[5]

The people of God want to be taken seriously, to know that this covenant to be God's people really matters to them and to the whole world. That is what is at the heart of strengthening the people of God for engagement in God's mission. Those whom the church asks and trains to be its leaders can do the very most when they expect and work toward the time when:

- each Christian sees self as a minister, experiencing being chosen by God for God's service;
- each Christian is engaged in God's service with creativity and faith, not fear;
- each person whom God possesses may be in ministry with Jesus Christ wherever that may be.

7

Engaging All God's People in Ministry

The community of Jesus Christ is called to be the leaven that stimulates the transformation of the world to the reign of God. That leaven requires certain conditions if it is to be kept alive and active. These cannot be fulfilled by admonitions from the pulpit or even national and regional programs, but only by thoughtful leadership of each local congregation.

In this chapter we will consider several conditions essential to engaging all God's people in ministry. First, the congregation members can be encouraged to identify their particular gifts and to see how these gifts can be used in ministry in the congregation and community. We shall then look at some ways congregations have organized themselves to enable persons to exercise their gifts for ministry. One way people have of relating their individual experiences to the larger context of their lives is by telling stories. Therefore, we shall suggest ways that people can be helped in recovering and telling their story. Also, those who minister appreciate clear guidelines that validate what they do as they use their gifts. We shall consider three essential elements in validation—authorization, accountability, and affirmation. Finally, we shall consider the role of the ordained leadership in a congregation committed to enabling all of its members to engage in ministry.

MATCHING GIFTS AND TASKS
One of the primary functions of a congregation is to aid its members in identifying and using their gifts. God gives each person unique gifts.

Because these gifts are God given, they must not be wasted. This is true for both laity and the ordained leadership. Recently I heard a laywoman say that although there was a lot of talk about gifts for ministry, what she needed was "help in focusing on my gifts for ministry and how they can be used in places other than the church. I need to know that my gift for administration is a spiritual gift, and I need that affirmation from my pastor and my church."

John Koenig has given us a helpful model for the task of matching gifts with the tasks of ministry to be done (see Figure 1). God gives both gifts and tasks. Sometimes we know that we have gifts but do not know how to use them. At other times we are presented with tasks that seem beyond us, yet we discover unknown gifts as we do them. The broken line between gifts and tasks represents the ongoing search to link the two. The arrows going to and from God indicate that this linking process always needs to happen in dialogue with God who is giver of both gift and tasks.[1]

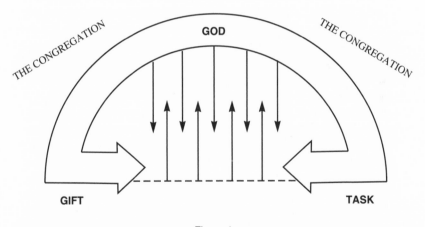

Figure 1

A California laywoman, Barbara Garrett, has suggested that a circle be envisioned around this linking process to represent the community of the church. She believes and has experienced the ministry of the local congregation as support and evoker of the match of gifts and tasks for each of its members.

Sometimes persons are clear about the gifts they have been given but have no idea of how they might use these gifts. Sometimes certain ministry tasks need to be done in a particular place or time, but no thought has been given about the gifts needed for those tasks or the persons available who might have those gifts. At other times, after a task has been done, people are amazed to realize that it was done by a person with just the necessary gifts whom no one, including that person, had ever suspected God had blessed in that way.

What are some ways for the congregation to proceed with this ministry of matching gifts and tasks?

Several exercises have been developed to help persons become aware of their God-given gifts. One set is based on the understanding that God gives each person talents and abilities that become spiritual gifts as one recognizes that these gifts have been given us by God to be used for God's purposes. We can encourage people to think about the things they have accomplished of which they were proud, which they did well, and which they enjoyed doing.[2]

In using this exercise I have found people more open to identifying talents and abilities when I begin by asking them about their accomplishments before they were six years old and those in the last six months. Then I suggest that people list four to ten accomplishments from the course of their lifetime. After they have made their lists, they are to examine several accomplishments and analyze exactly what they did to achieve them. It is in this analysis and in comparing the steps they took in each that they begin to see their own gifts. The third step in the process is mutual sharing of this work in a small group of two or three others. As each person tells his or her story, the others can assist in identifying gifts used, ones of which the teller is aware and needs confirmation and those that have never been recognized.

A similar structured exercise begins with persons identifying the times when they have felt most alive and then listing what they were doing in those times. Persons can choose several items out of this list to share with others.

Such gift identity exercises are best done in groups of Christian companions, not necessarily people who know us well, but those who can help us be honest and realistic about our gifts. They can help us name the gifts we do have, acknowledge those we do not have, then suggest ways to use our gifts.

Other exercises for identifying gifts are those based on the lists of spiritual gifts given by Paul in 1 Cor. 12:8-10 and Romans 12:6-8. Have people search, individually and in groups, to see which gifts they have been given. In such identification we need the help of others, for often Christians find it difficult to accept that God has truly gifted them. A false humility too often affirms the gifts of others but cannot accept one's own.

As people begin to name some of their gifts, they also need to explore the way in which they can use their gifts in ministry. The study of Mark 1:14-39 suggested in chapter 2 can be used here. Several of Jesus' ministries recorded in this passage can be chosen for further study. Such questions can be asked about each of these ministries as:

- Where today do we need the ministry of teaching or of touching or of telling the evil spirits to be quiet or of other ministries Jesus did?
- What gifts are needed for each of these ministries?
- Who among us has had such gifts affirmed?

A congregation that is committed to assisting its members in identifying and using their gifts will build this process into its ongoing life. This presumes different ways of engaging persons in the congregation's work. For example, when a search is being made for persons to assist in educational ministry, it is important to look for persons who have rich resources of Christian knowledge and experience of life to share, not just persons who are trained teachers. Matching gifts and tasks will require stated times for reviewing the ministries persons have been doing. Without such expected evaluation, persons can get stuck in a task year after year with their gifts stifled.

Periodic evaluation of the ministry of the whole congregation is important too. As part of that review there needs to be naming of the great variety of ministries that have been done in, through, outside, and to the congregation during that period. This review should include the ministry done by the ordained leadership and the laity from the youngest to the oldest and by those who have been part of the congregation but have left it for whatever reason since the last review. Identifying such ministries requires stretching of imaginations, finding ways to ensure that list goes beyond the traditional or the obvious or the customary. The persons named need to be made aware of the link between their gifts and the tasks of ministry.

Probably such naming is most powerful when it is celebrated in the worship of the people of God, for that is the act by which we are remembered, in which we realize our wholeness individually and corporately, and renew our vision for engagement in God's mission.

FORMATION OF THE CONGREGATION FOR MINISTRY

As there have been many varieties of ministry throughout the history of the Christian church, there have also been many different models for the formation of the congregation. The architecture of church buildings and liturgical patterns give us some clues about these forms. Also these models are reflected in the stated purposes of the congregation, the qualities and achievements that are honored, the way leaders are chosen and interact with members, the symbols and signs that are used in communication, the actual workings of the whole and of each part of the congregation. In chapter 1 we described several biblical metaphors of the church, focused on using to the full the gifts of all of its members, or alternatively focused on doing the jobs in the local congregation. Ernie Cordier has suggested that the congregation is to be a "ministry-factory which, operating in the name of our Lord and seeking out His will in all these matters, detects needs, empowers ministers, then celebrates and gives thanks for everything that happens in the divine dance that ensues."[3]

As we survey the various ways in which churches have organized for ministry, certain recurring patterns or models can be discerned. The model a congregation chooses will depend very much on how its leadership and its members define and understand the purpose of the church in that place. One model of the church could be called a *slot model* or a *structured organization model*. In such congregations mission is defined by what has always been done and what has always been assumed to be God's will. The various jobs in the church are defined in terms of this stated mission (Sunday school teachers, church council members, maintenance persons, etc.), and then "warm bodies" are sought to fill these slots. The model of mission defines the kinds of gifts that are needed.

Another model is the *living cell model*. Many people who are experienced in strengthening laity in ministry suggest that the leaven of transformation of the world to the reign of God is most alive and active in small groups of Christians. These groups work within and through and outside the institution of the church. A healthy, fertile congregation is able to support and sustain any number of small ministry groups or support groups for individuals involved in varieties of ministries. Many mustard plants can grow in good soil.

People are brought together on the basis of their gifts, commitments, and present ministries. As new persons enter the community and as present members find new gifts, the congregation's mission is continuously changing—developing new ministries, strengthening some traditional ones, dropping those that no longer can be sustained. The congregation ought to be a safe place to try out ideas, see if they work, and if necessary, go back to the planning stage to try again. The congregation is the place where people who might otherwise feel isolated in their ministry can come together for support and affirmation. A fertile congregation is a place to share knowledge, experience, and differing perspectives. Above all, the congregation is the place of common understanding to which God-called people come week by week to praise God and to offer celebrations and repentance for the ministry done or left undone. They are then sent out again with new power to be leaven for transformation.

The mission of the congregation is defined by the gifts of this gathering of God's people. It is God who gives the gifts and God who intends that they all be used for God's mission. In using God's gifts, we come to understand God's mission.

In the community of Jesus Christ, Jesus—not the pastor—is at the center of its life together. Although probably it will and should make use of the learnings from social sciences and community organization, this community takes its structure from the imperatives proclaimed by the gospel. We can picture it like a living cell. The nucleus, Jesus, gives the cell direction and life.

Another model of mission that has been developing in recent years, particularly in Latin America, is the *base community model*. The basic unit is the small Bible study group. Group members are challenged on the basis of their Bible study to look at present conditions. They ask what situations, problems, and crises are impinging on lives in their congregation, community, neighborhood, town, city, or nation. Then they reflect on what the Bible says to them about what they can do in each situation. Just as their reflection is based on their experience, they then are challenged to act on the basis of their reflection.

REMEMBERING AND TELLING STORIES

Sharing stories of the ministries we have received from others or have observed others doing is often helpful in determining how we can best use our gifts in ministry. Others may have perceived ministries we have done but are unaware of; we need to hear stories from those we have served.

Remembering is essential to the sharing of stories. It is an act in which we all can take part. Active remembering creates its own energy, to which all those who have been caught up in tracing their family's story can attest. We have seen persons "stand tall" as they discover who they are now because of those who have gone before. Sometimes this new knowledge is painful, sometimes it is glorious, always it is a mix, always it gives us the opportunity to make new decisions about who we shall be.

Further, there is a profoundly theological reason for engaging laypersons in remembering history. John Booty has said, "To be a Christian is to remember. . . ."[4] Christian remembering is really re-membering, becoming aware that we are parts of a larger community, members one of another. We need to know that we stand within a great "cloud of witnesses," those who came before us and those living today in many different places. Coming together week by week as Christians is an act of re-membering. For many Christians this happens in the Eucharist, which is primarily an act of re-membering, a sacrament of being rebound to God and each other through the body and blood of Christ. For other Christians, this re-membering happens in the common reception of the Word of God or in the silence of corporate prayer. In whatever circumstance, it can happen only when we are reaching out to know those with whom we are being re-membered. To be put together as whole people necessitates our knowing those with whom we are re-membered. Our worship and our life as Christians depend on our engagement in learning the stories of those who went before and those who are being the body of Christ with us today.

Some of us like to engage in compiling genealogies. It is good to engage the gifts of many persons in our church communities in exploring the genealogies of our own congregations. Searching for the circumstances in which our church family was formed; finding the stories of the first members; picturing ways in which this congregation has used its gifts to carry out God's mission in this place; tracing the roots of this congregation to other places, even other countries and other times—all these are ways to mine the stories of the ministries of men and women in our places.

Persons in different home and work and neighborhood places can find stories of others who have lived in similar places. For example, a group of Christian teachers or lawyers or musicians might find out all they can about Christians who have lived and served in these places before. Who were they? How did they fulfill their vocation to ministry? What difficulties did they face?

A group of young people could ask what part young people have had in the whole Christian story. In chapter 3, we mentioned Maximilian, a conscientious objector against army service in the third century. Who are other young Christians who have been conscientious objectors? What were the consequences of their decisions? What were the results? How have other young people brought together their commitment to God and their loyalty to their country, their people?

Today a widely used method for engaging in remembering is doing oral histories. This is a way to collect the stories of people living today whose lives reach quite far back into the past and are therefore a rich heritage for us. Some years ago Eliot Wigginton, a teacher in an Appalachia high school, worked with his students to collect the oral histories of people who live in those mountains. *Foxfire One*, *Two*, and *Three* are collections of these histories and give us some ideas of the richness of this method.[5] Several books and guides are available to help us become "oral historians."[6]

Just finding the stories is not enough. We need to tell the stories, visualize the stories, participate in the celebration of the stories so that we may have the power of being re-membered. The very success of the medium of television, especially historical dramas and even soap operas, points to the longing we all have to hear the stories of the way others have lived in the circumstances of their lives. However, the church has been so tied to the communication of the gospel through the printed word that we have been slow to share in other ways the wonderful stories of our heritage.

Telling stories can be done by using many different gifts of people in our community—the bodily and verbal skills of the traditional storyteller and the movements of dance; the art of painting, sculpture, poster-making, and photography; the musical gifts of composers and performers; video and movie-making and drama.

We need to use all the varieties of times and places where Christians gather to tell the stories. Our worship can be a time when our stories are interwoven with the telling of the Christian story.

Stories are an important part of our educational methodology. It has been in the small groups around campfires, family gatherings, and council meetings that the Hebrew tradition and much of the Christian tradition have been handed down over the centuries. We need to use those times and find others in which we can tell the stories we have received and those we are now finding ourselves. We need to nurture our children to be storytellers as well. Some living history will become treasure handed down by the Christian family as powerful stories to aid those whom God will call to be the *laos*, the people of God.

VALIDATING THE MINISTRY OF GOD'S PEOPLE

Three elements are essential in a congregation structured to strengthen the ministry of the people of God—authorization, accountability, and affirmation.

Very often, when prospective seminary students were asked why they wanted to be ordained, they would say they wanted authorization for doing pastoral work, especially visiting persons in the hospital. Some had the idea that a clerical collar or the title "Reverend" would give them permission and respect that was not available to them as laypersons.

Probably they were right, for society at large and many in the churches do not recognize or accept the ministry of the laity as "real ministry."

Therefore, the congregation has to work consistently toward ways to *authorize* the ministry of each person and of the people of God as a whole. Crucial to this is the growing understanding of baptism as the "ritual symbol through which God calls us individually and corporately, as God's ministers."[7] Is baptism celebrated in the congregation with the joy and seriousness that is usually reserved for the ordination of "the minister"? Do we encourage people to remember the anniversaries of their baptism and those of others?

What pictures of the church do we portray in the language of our liturgies and rites, in our congregational communications, in our personal language? Do our words reflect the recognition of the laity as persons who are given authority for ministry?

Each Christian must also believe that wherever and whatever possibilities for ministry are given, these are done on behalf of the whole church. The ministry of parents in a home matters to all the Christian community; so does the ministry of the manager in the office, the salesperson at the checkout counter, the teenager on the ball team. The congregation needs to structure ways in which Christians can give an account of the ways in which their ministry is being done in the place where each is. That too will require expansion of all traditional stereotypes about ministry.

Are there ways to inform the world outside the church about the authorization given to the laity for ministry? For example, if laypersons are going to visit in homes, nursing homes, and hospitals, how does the congregation tell the world they come as the ministers of the whole church? Or what about persons who visit fellow Christians to work with them on their commitment of time and money and talents to the work of the congregation? When these ministers are ready to begin these specific ministries, there needs to be a communication from the whole congregation—not just the ordained leader—to tell the world that this minister comes representing them all.

We must create a mutual system of *accountability* for those who are to be sent out under the auspices of the congregation. They need to be chosen because they have the most suitable abilities, be given education and training for the task, and be expected and helped to grow through ongoing evaluation of their ministry. This review always includes the possibility of recognizing that one's gifts will be better used in a different ministry. The congregation has the right to hear from its ministers about what is happening in the places where they are ministering. Equally, each Christian has the right to be listened to by other Christians as he or she tells the story of his or her ministry.

Such accountability can give the most support when the expectations and marks of achievement for that ministry are discussed. For example, what might a particular Christian community expect of the ministry of a teacher "telling the good news" in the classroom? Can the congregation and the minister work toward some mutually accepted job descriptions for this ministry? Can they together define some measures by which both will know there has been some achievement in this ministry?

We also need ways to develop accountability for the ministry we do in our everyday lives. William Diehl writes:

> In the almost thirty years of my professional career, my church has never once suggested that there be any type of accounting of my on-the-job ministry to others. My church has never once offered to improve those skills which could make me a better minister, nor has it ever asked if I needed any kind of support in what I was doing.[8]

Mutual evaluation of those ministries done within and through the church and those done in our everyday lives must include celebration for all the wonderful ways in which those ministries have served God. This mutual evaluation must also include repentance by the congregation for the ways in which it has failed to affirm and support ministry. If there have been such failures, some changes in the attitudes and work of the congregation itself will likely be needed. This mutual evaluation must include ways in which the one ministering can be helped to become clearer about the failures in the ministry and have a way to repent of these.

Through such processes as these, small groups of Christians can keep the community of Jesus Christ active as the leaven of transformation in the world. In a group like this, Michael, the accountant mentioned in the introduction (p. 9), could find the companionship he is looking for in working out his Christian commitment in his work.

These processes should not be confined to the work of small groups. Such patterns of accountability—defining the work expectations, describing the measures of achievement, doing the ministry, and carrying through the steps of mutual evaluation and celebration—should be in place in the total life of the congregation. The professional staff should certainly be included in these activities. Such processes need careful planning and patient practice, as well as adjustment depending on the size and location of the congregation. The carrying out of these processes in both large and small groups in the Christian community strengthens all ministers and encourages such patterns in the many other communities to which they belong.

Both *authorization* and *accountability* of the ministry of all Christians would go far in strengthening laity in ministry. *Affirming* and *honoring* are also strengthening. As we structure the congregation for this end, we need to note carefully who and what we affirm and honor in ministry. Most congregations honor the ordained ministers—at the beginning of their ordination, on anniversaries, when they move on to other locations for their ministry. We honor the decision makers in the congregation, such as the council or board members, and those who give much money to the church. Sometimes we honor those whom the community has honored, those whose names are printed in the paper so that we are proud that they are our members. Do we honor those whose ministries among us are not so visible—the people who clean the church, the Sunday school teachers, the secretaries? Do we honor the people who are caring for aged or dying relatives? What about those Christians who are ostracized by society for saying hard truths that no one wants to hear? Do we honor parents who have successfully raised their children to adulthood and are now moving to a different location in their ministry? Each congregation can with imagination and forethought put into place the modes of affirmation that will have most meaning and give most power to all its ministers.

RESPONSIBILITIES OF ORDAINED LEADERSHIP

Whenever the church has moved toward affirmation of the laity's ministry, there has been a tendency to reject or demean the ordained leadership's ministry. This was true in France after the eighteenth-century revolution when the word *laic* came to mean "anticlerical." Such a suspicion and divisiveness have also been operative in the church in our own time.

It is not strange that this has happened at a time when the very existence and rationale for the church as an institution have been judged by society and often declared irrelevant. Nor is it surprising that the church's appointed leaders are searching for their role and significance in such a 490changing situation. And it is no wonder that the church has used much of its energy in the past fifty years in reviewing who and what its ministers are to be.

There is still much work to be done theologically and structurally on the work of the ordained leadership within the congregation. A working copy of a paper on baptism being prepared by the Committee to Study Baptism of the United Methodist Church proposes:

> From within the universal priesthood of all believers, God calls and the Church authorizes a special representative ministry. The vocation of those in representative ministry lies in focusing, modeling, supervising, shepherding, enabling, and empowering the general ministry of the Church. Their ordination to Word, Sacrament and Order or consecration is grounded in the same baptism which constitutes the calling of the general priesthood of all believers.[9]

While each part of the Christian community needs to work on its own theology of ministry, this Methodist statement is helpful in defining quite clearly the tasks of ordained leaders. This definition is supported by research done by the Vocation Agency of the United Presbyterian Church in 1978-79. This study asked, "What style of pastoral leadership has stimulated and developed ministries in congregations where there are relatively high levels of involvement of their members in ministry to one another and to the community?"[10]

The first of seven themes that characterized these "ministering congregations" and their pastoral leadership was a *sense of grace* at work. The members of these churches felt they were accepted and that the church believed in their potential. Along with this reassurance was also a sense that "it is okay to fail." Even so, the members felt an expectancy that they would take their church membership seriously. The pastors of these congregations did not receive any special status but shared with the members the sense of being vulnerable and needing God's grace.

The second of the recurring themes coming out of this research was the sense on the part of the members of the church that they were *part of a caring community*. They experienced participation in small groups "where people can participate in mutual support, where they develop trust and experience intimacy [and] . . . learn to share their vulnerabilities just as they have seen their pastors do." This caring love is taught through the sermons, worship, study groups, announcements, and even meeting agendas.

Third, the focus of these churches was not on programming stated activities to be staffed by the membership, but on *recognizing the gifts that people bring* to the ministry. The pastors knew their people well enough to guide them toward the kinds of service they would find fulfilling. The pastors encouraged the people to develop their gifts through accomplishing successive small, achievable steps.

Fourth, these congregations shared *a clear vision of mission*. This vision was reinforced regularly by the pastors through their preaching and teaching. Thus the people felt "a clear and consistent sense of direction, a strong sense of purpose, and a contagious feeling of identity."

Fifth, pastors and people together experienced *a high commitment to a shared ministry*. The pastors themselves had a high enough level of personal security that they could forgo the need to control. They encouraged increasing lay involvement. This openness was based on firm convictions about the biblical and theological affirmations undergirding the ministry of all of the people.

Related to shared ministry, the sixth characteristic was *a forceful collegial style*. The pastors had clear role expectations for themselves and the congregation, with a clear sense of what their own contribution should be. They expected the laity to take responsibility for the things that were rightfully theirs to handle, even to the point of being willing to let some efforts fail if the laity did not assume their responsibilities. Planning and decision making were done in such a way as to insure broad support for the ministries of the church. The pastors did not expect to be involved in everything. In fact, in one church, the pastor demonstrated his trust in the lay leadership by suggesting that its committees meet at the same time. Thus it was physically impossible for him to be present with all the committees as they did their work.

The final characteristic of these ministering congregations was a sense of *spiritual authenticity*. The people realized that the pastors were not trying to manipulate them to achieve an agenda set by the pastor. Rather, they were taken seriously and given the opportunity to develop their own gifts for ministry.

The leadership of the church's ordained ministers is an essential part of the church's total ministry. When we juxtapose the findings of this

Presbyterian study against our usual picture of church leadership and structure, we are moved again to say, "Your ministry is too small." There is so much more to do than we will ever do using the gifts of all of God's creation.

The style of pastoral ministry effective for strengthening laity in ministry that was identified in this Presbyterian study can be carried out in the context of different theologies of ministry and diverse cultural patterns. This study and more recent ones point to the need for strong pastoral leadership. However, the strength of such leadership lies in the pastor's reliance on God's power to lead step by step to understanding the gifts given by the Holy Spirit. The pastor is open to trying out many ways to use his or her gifts in strengthening and supporting the gifts of others for ministry.

Exercises and Practical Helps

In this section are several exercises and other practical helps that will aid in the study of the material in this book. Some of them can be used by the individual reader, and some can be used by a group of people studying together. The headings under each chapter will help you relate the exercises to the material under the same heading in the body of the book.

1: GOD'S CALL TO MINISTRY
Metaphors of Ministry
Ways to Explore Metaphors

1. Choose a biblical metaphor. Check cross references and, using a concordance, see how key words in this metaphor are used in other passages.

2. With several other persons, draw a large picture of this metaphor. Rather than drawing it, you may prefer to make a sculpture of it, using a variety of materials or even your own bodies. For example, one group of fifteen portrayed the body of Christ by all trying to hold on to one person and move as a body.

3. Impose a picture or sculpture of your own congregation on the picture of the metaphor you have created. Reflect on the similarities and differences between these two pictures.

Creating New Metaphors

1. Ask a group to suggest fillers for the blanks in these sentences:

The church is like a _____ because it is (does) _____

_____ .

Our congregation is like a _____ because it is (does) _____

_____ .

God's mission is like a _____ .

Talk about the metaphors or models that are created. What can we learn from them?

2. Choose an inanimate object as different as possible from the church/mission/ministry at hand.

How is the church/mission/ministry like this object? For example, how is the church like a motorcycle? Elicit all possible analogies.

Write a new description of church/mission/ministry, using insights from these analogies.

2: BIBLICAL MODELS OF MINISTRY

Using Our Imagination to Put Ourselves into the Story

1. *Play around with the possibilities.* This exercise is best done in a group, both to expand the supply of ideas and to show how important it is to have the gifts of all involved in the task. Make as long a list as possible of the different kinds of Jesus' different ministries as recorded in Mark 1:14-39. Then ask: What might be all the possible ways in which we could follow Christ's ministry of "walking" or "touching" or "discerning evil spirits," or some other ministry, in our community?

2. *Fantasies.* The practice of fantasizing, or day-dreaming, either individually or in groups, can give us new perspectives on relationships, life pilgrimages, and recurrent problems. To begin, we need to be comfortable and relaxed. When doing individual day-dreaming, it is helpful to begin with a specific situation. For example, pretend that you are one of the Israelites who came out of Egypt to find the Promised Land. It is ten years later. What do you think and do? Or, locate yourself on the road to Jericho when Jesus walked by. You hear him call your name. What do you do?

Group fantasies can be guided by one person who creates a story or suggests a number of stimuli to guide the members of the group in pretending. Or the fantasy could be created by one person beginning a story and others contributing to it as it goes along. Whatever mode is used, when it is finished, after ten to twenty minutes, take time to reflect on what has happened and to share and compare each other's dreams.

Using the Material on Biblical Models

This material is part of the store of resources to be used in strengthening laity in ministry.

The first step in using the material is to read and digest it ourselves in relation to our own ministry as ordained or lay leaders in the church. It will be fruitful for personal study but can be very productive when used with clergy groups, church staff, or an adult leadership team in the church. Preparation of this material for use with other groups will be valuable for your own understanding.

The next step is to ask in relation to the people with whom we minister: What material is needed and can be helpful for these people (especially considering different ages, learning abilities, etc.) at this time in our community and world, in our particular lives in this particular place?

Some of the environments in which the material might be used are: youth retreats; home Bible studies; bulletin boards; sermons; baptism or confirmation classes; visual or audio expressions such as paintings, music, banners, photographs, and videos; Sunday school curriculums; newsletter articles or parish letters; quiet time meditations; ministry support groups; adult forums; and judicatory, council, or vestry meetings.

The biblical material can be used in sections:

- Separate stories, each engaged in depth.
- A series of stories from an overall perspective.
- A comparison of similar levels in different stories.
- A comparison of today's telling of the story with its origins.
- A search for models and metaphors within the stories.
- The creation of models and metaphors to fit the stories.

Abraham, the Faithful Friend of God

1. What are the different stories of Abraham? Why might these particular stories have been kept and handed down?

2. What have we learned about God from the way God has been a friend to us?

3. How have we responded as friends of God?

4. What does it look like to be a friend of God today—in all parts of our daily lives—work; home; social, economic, and political life; leisure time?

5. How can others come to know God through the good news of our friendship with God?

6. What other parts of the story of Abraham are important for our understanding of who we are as the people of God today?

The Kingdom of Priests and a Holy Nation

1. Where do we see God leading people out of slavery today?

2. Who are the people today carrying on the mission of Moses?

3. How are the people of God today

- a holy nation?
- a royal priesthood?
- God's own people?

What are the limitations of these pictures as well as their possibilities?

4. Who are the people today who bear the responsibility of being faithful rulers—in government at every level, business, finance, law, family?

5. What is the responsibility of the people of God in building a nation?

6. How might we describe God's involvement in the world today?

Community Builders

1. How do we use all the varied gifts of people in our congregation for strengthening the people of God for ministry?

2. Is it helpful or faithful to the story to say that the work of the ordained is in the church and the work of the laity is in the world? What are some other ways to describe the mutual responsibilities of the people of God?

3. What do we do with people today who talk about the "end of the world"? Are visionaries important to our Christian community now?

4. What are the possibilities and needs for "nation-building" in our city, state, nation, and world at this time? How do we equip and support the people of God in our place in this ministry?

Jesus' Ministry

1. Make lists of all the different ministries we see Jesus doing and being.

2. How are these different ministries being carried on today?

3. Which of these ministries might we be doing where we are today?

4. What would the ministry of *touching* look like today?

5. How do we recognize today when people are *setting at liberty those who are oppressed?*

Witnesses of the Resurrection

1. Where do we see the power of God's resurrection in the world today—in our homes, our work, our cities and nation, the natural world?

2. What stories do we know of people telling the good news of Christ's resurrection—in the past, in the present? Who has told us the good news? How did they tell us and how did we hear it?

3. How might we tell others the good news of God's power to resurrect?

4. How might we tell it as children? as young people? as adults?

5. How would we tell it to children? young people? older people? men? women? homeless people? political leaders? prisoners?

6. What other pictures of the Christian community do we find in the writings of Paul and in the other epistles?

7. Who are traveling prophets today? How does our Christian community support them? How do they share their ministry with us?

8. Does our congregation include the central features of Christian community that Luke describes in Acts 2:42-47?

9. How do we show that we know that God can use small communities of believers, including ours, to turn the world upside down?

10. What are the different ways in which people in our congregation are being Jesus' disciples?

3: THE PEOPLE OF GOD IN HISTORY
Telling Stories to Strengthen Ministry

Telling the stories of family and tribe and nation is a very popular occupation. Therefore, it is important that we use our imagination to present this historical material in as many different ways as possible to engage Christians of all ages in learning the stories of their own faith family.

Surely these will include:

- Celebration of the "saints' in worship and congregational life;
- Music and art; that which we have received from others and that which we create ourselves;
- Telling the stories in sermons;
- Materials for education with children, youth, and adults;
- Background for congregational decision making;
- Pointers for challenging Christians to seek further understanding of their vocation today, using questions such as these:

What was the context in which these Christians lived out their baptismal promises?

How was their situation different from ours? How was it similar?

What can we learn from them about being faithful in the present time?

How does their story strengthen us and give us new vision for our ministry?

Further Explorations into the History of the Laity

Examine the effect of the increasing institutionalization of the church on the operation of the church as the royal priesthood. Note especially the widening of the conceptual and structural splits within the church— between the sacred and secular, the spirit and the flesh, the church and the world, ministers and people. Note also the split between the teachers and the taught, and between the governed and those who were governed and expected to pay. Was the twelfth-century statement by the canon lawyer Gratian a logical conclusion of this institutionalization: "There are two kinds of Christians, the clergy who are to be devoted to divine office and contemplation and to rule themselves, . . . and the other sort of Christians who are called 'lay folk' "? Would this summary apply today?

Learn about the athletes of God, the many men and women, mostly laypersons, who went into the desert from the cities in order to live more fully their commitment to God.

Study the development of the monastic movement. Learn about Benedict of Nursia, the "Patriarch of Western monasticism" who was a layman.[1] Read the rule he wrote for his community. How does the balance of prayer, study, and work in this rule give direction for the spirituality of the laity?

Study also the life of Francis of Assisi. In the beginning his order was mainly lay people and he always wore the tonsure of a layperson. However, the hierarchy in Rome persuaded him to be ordained a deacon for the sake of the order, and the next generation of Franciscans were mostly priests. Compare Francis with Origen and with other laypersons in the history of the church.

Observe how the rulers and nobility modeled the Christian lay life. Tell the stories of Charlemagne (A.D. 742-814) and Alfred the Great, King of Wessex (849-99).

WHAT IS THE MISSION OF THE CHURCH?	The mission of the church is to restore all people to unity with God and each other in Christ.		
	Places in our community where there is separation. (Give specific examples.)	What would we like the Christian community to be doing in this place? How could we help to bring unity with God and each other in Christ in this place? (Be specific.)	Who could help us in our mission in this place? (Give specific names.)
FAMILY			
EDUCATION			
GOVERNMENT			
BUSINESS/INDUSTRY			
COMMUNITY RELATIONSHIPS			
HEALTH/ENVIRONMENT			
RELIGION			

Figure 2

4: THE NATURE OF MINISTRY

The Ministry of Reconciliation

The chart (Figure 2) on page 102 can be used to help identify places where reconciliation is needed and what the Christian community can do in such instances.

Strengthening the Saints in the Ministry of Friendship

1. It is essential that we provide times and places for people to tell their stories. In the church we have to create these times and places, for such storytelling does not seem to happen by itself very often. Being truly inclusive involves not only changing liturgy and language but recognizing, honoring, and listening to diverse stories. The church wastes incredible amounts of energy and riches in listening to only a limited number of its members.

2. All the church's ordained and lay leaders need to experience for themselves and help others to experience as many possible views of the world as they can. Ecumenical events, interdenominational and interfaith, interage and intersex, intercultural and international—are all ways in which people can experience different views of the world.

3. An important teaching and preaching task is the exploration of what is meant by the words in the Creed: "We believe in the holy Catholic Church." What does this mean? What are the implications of our affirming this as individuals and as a community Sunday by Sunday?

4. The ancient sacramental act of Sharing the Peace (or the kiss of peace) has been restored to many Christian liturgies in the past fifty years. However, the people of God need continually to relearn the significance of this act and to reevaluate its use in their worship.

What do we think we are doing when we perform this act?

What does it commit us to do in our daily lives?

Is there anyone with whom or any time when we would refuse to give or receive the Peace?

How can we as a community be fully open to God unless we are open to the friendship of those in the pews around us? How can we ensure that there is a variety of persons in the pews around us?

5. The ministry of friendship is a ministry of hope. We can multiply the energy for hope through sharing in celebration. The congregational leaders, both ordained and lay, can provide encouragement, time, and space for celebration. Also, they are critical in linking people and resources for turning dreams into realities.

5: CONNECTING WITH THE PEOPLE
Issues Important to the Laity

It is important for church leaders to set up situations in which they can listen intentionally to laity. Interviews are a helpful tool for doing this.

Set up several interviews with several laypersons in your congregation or community. The questions adapted from Dr. Nelvin Vos's work on page 61 are a good format to follow for your first interviews. As you carry on more interviews, you will want to develop your own interview questions. It is important to structure the interview so that it will be distinguished from a pastoral or social visit. Some guidelines to follow are:

- Make an appointment with the interviewee and share your intention for the interview.
- Set a time limit; one-half hour ought to be enough.
- Decide how you are going to record the interviewee's responses. If you want to tape them, make sure to ask permission.
- Tell the interviewee what you intend to do with the material you collect.
- Take the time to reflect on the interviews, on both what you have learned and the way in which you have conducted the interviews.

The practice of interviewing is a worthwhile one to carry on throughout your leadership ministry.

Relating Theological Insights to Daily Occupations

Try out the affirmations of the Christian faith on pages 63-65 in your congregation.

- Focus on them in sermons.
- Ask lay people to work out case studies in which these affirmations are relevant or to write questions about them.
- Study newspaper, magazine, and journal articles and television programs for ways in which these affirmations are acknowledged, questioned, or refuted.

Theological Education of the Laity

Use the questions on page 66 as a guide and standard for all your congregation's educational ministry—children, youth, and adults.

Ask lay people of different ages:

How do you answer the question "Who is Jesus Christ?" (or any of the other questions)?

In what way does the life in this congregtion assist our people in answering the question "Who is Jesus Christ?" (or any of the other questions)?

How might we help each other answer this question in a more satisfactory way?

Clergy/Occupation Dialogues and Workplace Seminars

Find out ways to carry out these dialogues among people in your congregation and with clergy and laity in other congregations in your community. Probably clergy and lay leaders will have to initiate such dialogues and seminars, but it is critical to find ways in which laypersons become partners in the dialogue and the primary discussants in the seminars. Clergy and lay leaders need to be clear about their own roles in these processes and to share their understandings of their roles and gifts with the other participants.

6: STRENGTHENING THE SPIRIT FOR MINISTRY
Planning Worship to Meet Needs

Leaders of worship need to ask:

1. Are they themselves people who meet God in their lives so that they have experiences to share with others?

2. Is the worship of the congregation planned and conducted in such a way that people meet God there and so can recognize God in other places?

3. Are there special times such as retreats, quiet days, quiet hours, and times of silence planned in the ongoing program of the congregation in which people can experience meeting God?

4. Are the congregation's worship and program planned to be responsive to the gifts and needs of its members?

7: ENGAGING ALL GOD'S PEOPLE IN MINISTRY
Formation of the Congregation for Ministry

What models of the church are presently operating in your congregation? Compare these models with the models of the gifted community in Acts 2:42-47 and 1 Corinthians 12 and 14.

1. Which model does our congregation use?

2. Could we use more than one of these models at the same time?

3. What changes would we have to make if we were going to adopt a model different from the one we now use?

4. What leadership gifts would our congregation need to support a different model? Are these gifts available in our congregation?

Remembering and Telling Stories

To be remembered within our living Christian community today requires times and places in which we can share the stories of our own opportunities and experiences of responding to God's call in our daily lives. Here are some questions that can help us focus our sharing of these stories:

1. How do I spend most of each day that God is giving me?

2. How many people do I meet each day? What kind of "meeting" do I have with them? How do I use the gifts God has given me in my relationships with them?

3. What kinds of problems, tensions, decisions do I have to face every day? How do I work with these?

4. What are the times when I want to celebrate in my day-to-day living? How do I celebrate these?

5. How do I bring what I do in church into my ministry in my daily life? How do I bring what I do in my daily life into the worship and life of my church community?

6. What are new ways or places that God seems to be calling me to serve in my life situations?

Notes

Introduction

1. Yves M. J. Congar, O.P., *Lay People in the Church*, trans. Donald Attwater (Westminster, Md.: Newman, 1956; 1953, printed in France); Hendrik Kraemer, *A Theology of the Laity* (London: Lutterworth, 1958, and Louisville: Westminster/ John Knox, 1958).

2. Michael Macey, "Christianity at Work" in *Slimline* (South London Industrial Mission: London, November 1987), 3-4.

1: God's Call to Ministry

1. Originally the word *Israel* was a religious term. It referred to the "tribes united by the covenant." This changed after the division of Solomon's kingdom in about 922 B.C. Bernard W. Anderson, *Understanding the Old Testament*, 3d ed. (Englewood Cliffs, N.J.: Prentice-Hall, 1975), 233n.

2. R. H. Faulkner, *The National Baptist Churchman's Handbook* (Marian, Ind.: Bainbridge, 1982), 52.

3. Anne Field, O.S.B., *New Life* (London and Oxford: Mowbray, 1980; original 1978 ed. by Servant, Ann Arbor, Mich.), 189-92.

4. Aidan Kavanagh, "The Three Days," in *The Three Days: Parish Prayer in the Pascal Triduum*, ed. by Gabe Huck (Chicago: Liturgy Training Publications, 1978), 107-10. Originally an article in *Liturgy 1970 Magazine*. Reprinted with permission of Aidan Kavanagh, all rights reserved.

5. *The Book of Common Prayer* (New York: Seabury, 1979), 229-308.

6. See Ruth A. Tucker, *From Jerusalem to Irianjaya: A Biographical History of Christian Missions* (Grand Rapids, Mich.: Academic Books, 1983), 115.

2: Biblical Models of Ministry

1. William R. White, *Speaking in Stories* (Minneapolis: Augsburg, 1982), 22.

2. In *Webster's Third New International Dictionary* (Springfield, Mass.: G. and R. Merriam, 1966), p. 1281, the word *lay* is defined as "not of or from a particular profession . . . *unprofessional: common: ordinary*." In *The Oxford English Dictionary* (*OED*) (Oxford: Clarendon, 1989), 8:724, the word is defined as "not in orders." The *OED* also tells us that Tertullian, about 220, was the first to use the Latin word *clerus* for those whom 1 Peter 5:3 called "those in your charge," and Jerome followed Tertullian's use in the fourth century. From then on the use of the words *laity* and *clergy* to distinguish two kinds of Christians became more common until today when these are the accepted assumptions in the dictionaries' meanings. This book is one small piece in the whole movement to restore the meaning of *lay* to its rightful connection with the biblical understanding of "God's own people."

3. Ernesto Cardinal, *The Gospel in Solentiname,* vol. 1-4, trans. Donald D. Walsh (Maryknoll, N.Y.: Orbis, 1976-1981).

4. Shisaku Endo, *Silence,* trans. William Johnston (New York: Taplinger Publishing Co., 1980).

5. I owe much of the following material to John Koenig, *New Testament Hospitality* (Minneapolis: Fortress, 1985); and Robert J. Karris, "Missionary Communities: A New Paradigm for the Study of Luke-Acts" in *Catholic Biblical Quarterly*, 41, 1979, 80-97.

6. Koenig, *New Testament Hospitality*, 98.

3: The People of God in History

1. Stephen Charles Neill and Hans-Ruedi Weber, ed., *The Layman in Christian History* (Louisville: Westminster/John Knox, 1963).

2. *Christian Spirituality*, ed. Bernard McGinn, John Meyendorff, and Jean Leclerq (New York: Crossroad, 1987).

3. Wayne Meeks, *The First Urban Christians* (New Haven: Yale University Press, 1983); and Elisabeth Schüssler Fiorenza, *In Memory of Her* (New York: Crossroad, 1986).

4. Quoted in "The Ancient Church" by George Hunstone Williams in Neill and Weber, *The Layman in Christian History*, 49.

5. Tertullian, *Apologeticum* 39, quoted in Williams, "The Ancient Church," in Neill and Weber, *The Layman in Christian History*, 45.

6. Yves M. J. Congar, O.P., *Lay People in the Church*, trans. Donald Attwater (Westminster, Md.: Newman, 1956; 1953, printed in France), 7-9.

7. Claire Cross, *Church and People, 1450-1660* (Glasgow: William Collins & Son, Fontana paperbacks, 1979), 17.

8. Martin Luther, "Concerning Christian Liberty," from *Luther's Primary Works*, ed. Henry Wace and C. A. Buchheim (London: Hodder and Stoughton, 1896), as quoted in *Great Voices of the Reformation*, ed. with commentaries by Harry Emerson Fosdick (New York: The Modern Library, 1952), 86.

9. See *Women in Reformation and Counter Reformation Europe*, ed. Sherrin Marshall (Bloomington, Ind.: Indiana University Press, 1989).

10. Quoted in Peter Meinhold, "Modern Europe, 1800-1962," in Neill and Weber, *The Layman in Christian History*, 175-76.

11. Program for the Samba-Likhaan Groundbreaking Ceremony, January 6, 1990, Cathedral Heights Compound, 275 E. Rodriguez, Sr., Boulevard, Quezon City, The Philippines.

12. E Mackerchar, *Mary Reed of Chandag* (London: The Mission to Lepers, 1899).

4: The Nature of Ministry

1. *The Book of Common Prayer* (New York: Seabury, 1979), 855.

2. R. H. Faulkner, *The National Baptist Churchman's Handbook* (Marion, Ind.: Bainbridge, 1982), 53.

3. Aelred of Rievaulx, *Spiritual Friendship* (c. 1160), trans. Mary Eugenia Laker, SSND (Washington, D.C.: Cistercian Publications, Consortium Press, 1974), 1:70.

4. The ideas in this section were much helped by an article by Sandra M. Schneiders, "The Foot Washing: John 13:1-20: An Experiment in Hermeneutics," in *The Catholic Biblical Quarterly*, 43, 1981, 76-92.

5. William Diehl, *Christianity and Real Life* (Philadelphia: Fortress, 1976), 49.

6. W. H. Gardner and N. H. MacKenzie, eds., *The Poems of Gerard Manly Hopkins*, 4th ed. (London: Oxford University Press, 1967), poem 57 on p. 90.

5: Connecting with the People

1. Renae Hyer, "The Laity in Business and Corporate Life." *Laity Exchange,* 1979.

2. See Nelvin Vos, *Monday's Ministries* (Philadelphia: Parish Life Press, 1979), 4.

3. *San Francisco Chronicle*, March 4, 1989, B-3.

4. "Discipleship and Citizenship in the Workplace," an address on the occasion of The Annual Mark Gibbs Lectureship of the Vesper Society Group at Fuller Theological Seminary, Pasadena, California, April 27, 1990. In cooperation with Fuller Theological Seminary Marketplace Ministries/InterVarsity Christian Fellowship, 13.

5. Publishers of these programs are: Kerygma Program, Suite 2217, 300 Mt. Lebanon Blvd., Pittsburgh, PA 15234; The Bethel Series, Adult Christian Education Foundation, 313 Price Place, Box 5305, Madison, WI 53705; University of the South, Education for Ministry, School of Theology Extension Center, Sewanee, TN 37375-9900.

6. *Initiatives*, March 1989, published by the National Center for the Laity, 1 E. Superior St., #311, Chicago, IL 60611.

7. The Zadok Centre, "La Verna," 39 Sackville Street, Kew Victoria 3101 Australia.

6: Strengthening the Spirit for Ministry

1. See *The Interpreter's Dictionary of the Bible* (Nashville: Abingdon, 1962), 4:135.

2. Charles Péguy, "Sleep," in *God Speaks*, trans. and intro. by Julian Green (New York: Pantheon Books, 1945), 22-23.

3. Thich Nhat Hanh, *The Miracle of Mindfulness* (Boston: Beacon Press, 1975), 85.

4. Jean Haldane, *Religious Pilgrimages and Church Socialization* (Jean Haldane, 1435 Fourth St., S.W., Washington, D.C. 20024, 1974), 1.

5. Patrick M. Arnold, "The Masculine Voice in Spirituality," *Laity Exchange*, no. 26, 1985.

7: Engaging All God's People in Ministry

1. John Koenig, *Charismata: God's Gifts for God's People* (Louisville: Westminster/John Knox, 1978), 147.

2. See Jean M. Haldane, *Ministry Explorations: A Total Ministry Support System* (Seattle, Wash.: Renewal Press, 1981), proof ed., 164-70.

3. Ernie Cordier, "The Past Is Prologue: Raising Issues in Lay Ministry Management," in *Action Information* (Washington, D.C.: Alban Institute, vol. 16, no. 5 (September/October, 1990), 20-22.

4. John Booty, *The Church in History* (New York: Seabury, 1979), 4.

5. *Foxfire Books* 1-9 (Garden City, N.Y.: Anchor, 1972, 1973, 1975, 1977, 1979, 1980, 1982, 1984, 1986). See also Eliot Wigginton, *Foxfire: Twenty-five Years* (Garden City, N.Y.: Anchor, Doubleday, 1991).

6. See *Women's Words: A Feminist Practice of Oral History*, ed. Sherna B. Gluck and Daphne Patal (New York: Routledge, Chapman, and Hall, 1991), especially "Learning to Listen: Interview Techniques and Analyses," by Kathyrn Anderson and Dana C. Jack, 11-26. Two journals will also be helpful—*Oral History Review* and *International Journal of Oral History*. A useful film is "An Oral Historian's Work" by Dr. Edward Ives. Sheldon Weiss Production, Rte. 175, Blue Hill Falls, ME 04615.

7. *The Book of Discipline*, 1988, par. 105, The United Methodist Church.

8. William Diehl, *Christianity and Real Life* (Philadelphia: Fortress, 1976), v-vi.

9. "By Water and the Spirit: A Proposed United Methodist Understanding of Baptism," The Report of the Baptism Study Committee of the United Methodist Church, August 1991, sec. 6, 2. This report was submitted to the General Conference of the United Methodist Church in May 1992 for acceptance as a study guide.

10. Donald P. Smith, "Shared Ministry," *Theology Today*, vol. 36 (October 1979), 3.

Exercises and Practical Helps

1. E. A. Livingstone, ed., *The Concise Oxford Dictionary of the Christian Church* (Oxford: Oxford University Press, 1977), 57.